C000056169

Que® Quick Reference Series

WordPerfect® Quick Reference

Developed by
Que Corporation

Que Corporation
Carmel, Indiana

Library of Congress Catalog Number: 88-61932

ISBN 0-88022-370-7

91   90   9

Interpretation of the printing code: the rightmost
double-digit number is the year of the book's printing;
the rightmost single-digit number, the number of the
book's printing. For example, a printing code of 89-4
shows that the fourth printing of the book occurred in
1989.

This book is based on WordPerfect Version 5.0.

Que Quick Reference Series

The *Que Quick Reference Series* is a portable resource of essential microcomputer knowledge. Whether you are a new or experienced user, you can rely on the high-quality information contained in these convenient guides.

Drawing on the experience of many of Que's best-selling authors, the *Que Quick Reference Series* helps you easily access important program information. Now it's easy to look up often-used commands and functions for 1-2-3, WordPerfect 5, Microsoft Word 5, MS-DOS, and dBASE IV as well as programming information for C, Turbo Pascal, and QuickBASIC 4.

Use the *Que Quick Reference Series* as a compact alternative to confusing and complicated traditional documentation.

The *Que Quick Reference Series* also includes these titles:

Publishing Director
   Scott N. Flanders

Product Director
   Karen A. Bluestein

Senior Editor
   Lloyd J. Short

Editorial Assistants
   Debra S. Reahard
   Ann K. Taylor

Production
   Composed on a Macintosh II using PageMaker 3.0

Trademark Acknowledgments
   IBM, IBM PC AT, and Personal System/2 are
   registered trademarks, and IBM PC XT is a trademark
   of International Business Machines Corporation.

   Lotus and 1-2-3 are registered trademarks of Lotus
   Development Corporation.

   Macintosh is a registered trademark of Apple
   Computer, Inc.

   MS-DOS is a registered trademark of Microsoft
   Corporation.

   PageMaker is a registered trademark of Aldus
   Corporation.

   WordPerfect is a registered trademark of WordPerfect
   Corporation.

Table of Contents

Introduction

WordPerfect Quick Reference offers you the instant quick reference information you need as you create, format, edit, proofread, and print WordPerfect documents—documents ranging from simple memos to complex and lengthy legal briefs. This book is a compilation of the most frequently used information from Que's best-selling publications on WordPerfect 5.

WordPerfect Quick Reference is divided into sections by tasks, or applications. One section, for example, is called "Columns." If you are in the middle of a project and can't remember how to create newspaper-style columns of text, turn to the "Columns" section. Another section is called "Printing." In this section you will find the basic steps needed to complete your WordPerfect printing tasks. Each section of this quick reference takes you step-by-step through the features, functions, and commands WordPerfect 5 users employ every day.

WordPerfect Quick Reference provides clear, easy instructions for quickly performing basic word-processing tasks, but it is not intended to replace the comprehensive information presented in a full-size tutorial or a less portable reference for WordPerfect 5. You should supplement this quick reference with Que's *Using WordPerfect 5* and *WordPerfect QueCards*.

Now you can put essential information at your fingertips with *WordPerfect Quick Reference*—and the entire *Que Quick Reference Series*.

Adding Text

WordPerfect normally operates in *Insert mode*. Insert mode means that as you type, the new characters are inserted, and existing text moves forward and is automatically formatted. As you type, sentences may push beyond the right margin and may not immediately wrap to the next line. Don't worry. The lines adjust as you continue to type.

Typeover mode generally is used if you have typed text incorrectly. For example, you probably would select Typeover mode to replace text if you mistakenly had typed the name *Jane* instead of *Dane*.

Before you add text, remember that Typeover mode *replaces* your original text; Insert mode *adds* new text to existing text.

To add text by using Insert mode

1. Place the cursor where you want to insert new text.

2. Type the new text.

To add text by typing over existing text

1. Place the cursor where you want the new text to begin.

2. Press **Ins** to turn off Insert mode. The following indicator appears at the lower left of your screen:

   ```
   Typeover
   ```

3. Type the new text.

4. Press **Ins** again to return to Insert mode.

Block Command

The most powerful and flexible command in
WordPerfect is the Block command (Alt-F4, or F12 on
the Enhanced Keyboard). This command is used with
other WordPerfect features to block (isolate) specific
segments of text so that only the blocked text is affected
by those features.

A block can be as short as a single character or word or
as long as an entire document. Blocks can be a single
character, a single word, a phrase, a sentence, a
paragraph, a page, a column, a rectangle of text of any
size, or a document.

On your computer screen, blocked text appears
highlighted. After the text is highlighted, it is ready for
the second step in a variety of operations.

Some WordPerfect features cannot be used with the
Block command. For example, to change margin
settings in a portion of your document, the Format Line
command is used, not the Block command.

Defining a Block

Before you do anything to a block of text, you must tell
WordPerfect exactly what portion of the text is to be
affected. To do so, you first use the Block command to
define the block of text by highlighting it on-screen.

To Define a Block of Text

1. Move the cursor to the character that begins the
    block of text you want to define.

2. Press Alt-F4, or F12, to begin the Block command.

The following message flashes in the lower left corner of your screen:

```
Block on
```

3. Move the cursor to the right until the last character in the block of text is highlighted.

Use the cursor-arrow, PgDn, PgUp, and GoTo (Ctrl-Home) keys to move the cursor. You can move the cursor either forward or backward to define text. The highlight moves with the cursor.

4. Press the key that invokes the feature you plan to use on the highlighted block of text.

If the feature you've selected will not work with the Block command, WordPerfect signals you with a beep.

To back out of the feature while the block is highlighted, press **F1** (**Cancel**), or **Alt-F4** or **F12** (**Block**), to turn off the Block command. The `Block on` message disappears, and the text no longer appears highlighted. The cursor remains at the end of the block (where it was when you finished highlighting).

Some commands, such as Block Print or Block Delete, require confirmation. If a `Y/N` prompt appears at the lower left of the screen, complete the next step.

5. Press **Y** for Yes or press **N** for No.

The feature you've selected in Step 4 executes only on the highlighted block of text.

To rehighlight the block for use with another feature, or to restore highlighting if you accidentally turn off the Block feature, complete the next steps.

6. Press **Alt-F4** or **F12** (**Block**).

7. Press **Ctrl-Home** (**GoTo**) to activate the GoTo command.

8. Press **Ctrl-Home** (**GoTo**) again to return to the beginning of the block.

Block highlighting disappears automatically as soon as the task (such as move, copy, or bold) is completed.

Moving a Block

Moving a block of text is a "cut-and-paste" operation. Using WordPerfect, you simply define the block, cut it from its current location, and move it to a new location in your document. The block is erased from its previous location and appears in the new location. The new location can even be in another document.

To move a block of text

1. With **Alt-F4** or **F12**, define the block of text you want to move.

2. Press **Ctrl-F4** (**Move**) to display the Move menu:

```
Move: 1 Block; 2 Tabular Column; 3
Rectangle: 0
```

3. Press **1** or **B** to select Block.

4. Press **1** or **M** to select Move. WordPerfect cuts the defined block, and it disappears from the screen. Don't worry; a copy of the defined block is stored in temporary memory. WordPerfect displays the following message:

```
Move cursor; press Enter to
retrieve.
```

5. Move the cursor to the location in your document where you want the cut block to appear.

6. Press **Enter** to insert the block at the new location.

Copying a Block

When you copy a block of text, WordPerfect places into memory a duplicate of the block you've defined. You then can retrieve this block from memory and insert the block at another location in your document or in another document. To copy a block of text, you use the Block command (Alt-F4 or F12) with the Move command (Ctrl-F4).

To copy a block of text

1. With **Alt-F4** or **F12**, define the block to be copied.

2. Press **Ctrl-F4** (**Move**) to display the Move menu.

3. Press **1** or **B** to select Block.

4. Press **2** or **C** to select Copy. The highlighting disappears, and the following message appears on-screen:

   ```
   Move cursor; press Enter to
   retrieve.
   ```

5. Move the cursor to the location in your document where you want the duplicate text to appear.

6. Press **Enter**

Deleting a Block

Block Delete is the most efficient way to delete more than one or two characters. In a few keystrokes, you can delete a sentence or three full pages of outdated text.

To delete a block of text

1. With **Alt-F4** or **F12**, define the block to be deleted.

2. Press the **Del** key or the **Backspace** key. The following prompt is displayed at the bottom left of your screen:

```
Delete Block? (Y/N) No
```

3. Press **Y**. (If you press **N**, you are returned to the highlighted text.) The block is deleted from your document.

You can delete as many, as three blocks and restore them all using the Undelete (F1) feature.

Restoring a Block

To restore deleted text

1. Press **F1** (**Cancel/Undelete**) to display the most recently deleted text. The following menu appears in the status line:

```
Undelete: 1 Restore; 2 Previous
Deletion: 0
```

2. Press **1** or **R** to restore the text to your document, or press **2** or **P** to display the previous deletion.

If the previous deletion is the text you want restored, press **1**; if not, press **2** again to view the third, and last, deletion.

Saving a Block

WordPerfect's Block Save function helps reduce the amount of work when you must type the same block of text in one document several times. With Save, you define the block of text you plan to use frequently, and then save the block to a separate file.

To save a block of text

1. With **Alt-F4** or **F12**, define the block you want to save.

2. Press **F10** (**Save**). The following prompt appears on-screen:

```
Block name:
```

3. Type the name of the file in which you want to save the block.

Select a file name that clearly identifies the block you are saving. Be sure to include a drive letter and path name before the file name if you want to save the block to a directory other than the directory you are working from.

4. Press **Enter**.

Printing a Block

Sometimes you will want to print only a single block of text from a document. Use the Block Print command to print part of your document.

To print a block of text

1. With **Alt-F4** or **F12**, define the block you plan to print.

2. Press **Shift-F7** (**Print**). The following prompt appears on-screen:

```
Print Block? (Y/N) No
```

3. Press **Y**.

Appending a Block

WordPerfect provides a simple way to add text to one document while you are working on another, using Block Append. With Append, the text is attached to the end of the document.

To append a block of text

1. With **Alt-F4** or **F12**, define the text you plan to append.

2. Press **Ctrl-F4** (**Move**).

3. Press **1** or **B** for Block.

4. Press **4** or **A** for Append. WordPerfect displays the following message:

   ```
   Append to:
   ```

5. Type the file name of the document to which you want to append the block. The block remains in your current document and is added to the end of your other document.

Changing Block Case

To change upper- or lowercase

1. With **Alt-F4** or **F12**, define the block you plan to change to upper- or lowercase letters.

2. Press **Shift-F3** (**Switch**) to display the following menu:

   ```
   1 Uppercase; 2 Lowercase: 0
   ```

3. Press **1** or **U** to change the block to uppercase letters, or press **2** or **L** to change the block to lowercase letters.

Centering a Block of Text

To center a block of text

1. With **Alt-F4** or **F12**, define the block of text you want to center.

2. Press **Shift-F6** (**Center**). WordPerfect displays the following prompt:

```
[Cntr]? (Y/N) No
```

3. Press **Y** to center the block. The block is centered between the left and right margins.

Enhancing a Block of Text

To boldface or underline a block of text

1. With **Alt-F4** or **F12** (**Block**), define the block of text you want to boldface or underline.

2. Press **F6** to turn on Bold, or press **F8** to turn on Underline.

If you want the block to be both boldfaced and underlined, highlight the block again by pressing **Alt-F4** or **F12** (**Block**), and then press **Ctrl-Home** (**GoTo**) twice. Press **F6** (**Bold**) or **F8** (**Underline**), depending on which you used the first time.

Cancel/Undelete

The Cancel/Undelete key (the F1 "oops" key) allows you to back out of a menu without making a selection or restore text you have mistakenly deleted.

When used as a cancel key, F1 cancels the most recent command and returns you either to the preceding menu or to your document. When used as an undelete key, F1 retrieves one of the last three items you've deleted. An *item* in this case means the characters (numbers, letters, or punctuation) deleted before moving the cursor. F1 always acts as an undelete key when a menu is not visible.

To back out of a menu

Some menus disregard your selections if you leave the menu by pressing the Cancel key (F1). These menus display a message that instructs you to leave the menu by pressing the Exit key (F7) if you want to save your selections in memory.

Press F1 (Cancel) to return to a preceding menu without making a choice from the current menu. When there is no preceding menu to which to return, you are returned to the current document.

Restoring Deleted Text

Press F1 (Cancel) to restore deleted text either to its original location or to another location.

Remember, however, that WordPerfect stores only the last three deletions. When you make a fourth deletion, the oldest of the three preceding deletions is erased from memory.

Deleted text is not saved when you exit WordPerfect. If you want to save text, you must paste it into a document and save the document.

To restore deleted text

1. Move the cursor to the location where the deleted item should reappear. If you have just deleted the text and want it returned to its original location, do not move the cursor.

2. Press F1 (Cancel) to display the Undelete menu and the text you last deleted. The last deletion shows as highlighted text at the cursor's location. At this point, you have three options: (a) press F1 (Cancel) if you want to return to typing without restoring the text; (b) press 1 or R for Restore if you want to

restore the deleted text to your document; or (c) press **2** or **P** for Previous Deletion until the text you want to restore is displayed, and then type **1** or **R** for Restore.

Centering Text

WordPerfect lets you center text instantly. You can center a line as you type it or after you've entered it. You also can center a page from top to bottom.

To center text that you are about to type

1. Move the cursor to the left margin of the line you want to center.

2. Press **Shift-F6** (**Center**). The cursor centers between the margins. As you type, the text adjusts to the left and to the right in order to stay centered.

3. Type your text and press **Enter**.

If you type more characters than will fit between the margins, the rest of the text moves to the next line. Only the first line is centered. To center several lines, use the Block Center function.

To center an existing line of text

1. Place the cursor at the left margin of the line of text you want to center.

2. Press **Shift-F6** (**Center**) to move the text to the center of the screen.

3. Press ↓.

The text appears centered on-screen. To center an existing line of text, the line must end with a hard return [HRt].

To center text around a specific point

1. With the cursor in the line to be centered, press Alt-F3, or F11 and make sure there are no codes, characters, or spaces on the line.

2. Press Alt-F3, or F11 again to leave the Reveal Codes screen.

3. Press the space bar to move the cursor to the character position on which you want to center the text.

4. Press Shift-F6 (Center) and type your text, and then press Enter.

The text is centered on the character position. You cannot center previously typed text around a specific point.

When you center a page top to bottom, the setting applies to just one page—the page where you make the setting. The end of a centered page can be defined either by a soft page break or by a hard page break. Ending the centered page with a hard page break ensures that it never accidentally merges with the next page. Usually a page centered top to bottom is a separate page, and shorter than the other pages in the document.

To center text between the top and bottom margins

1. Place the cursor at the top left margin of the page.

2. Press **Shift-F8 (Format)** to display the Format menu.

3. Press **2** or **P** to display the Format: Page menu.

4. Press **1** or **C** for Center Page.

5. Press **F7 (Exit)** to return to your document.

Although the page doesn't move on-screen, it will be centered when you print your document. If you change your mind, use Reveal Codes to delete the [Center Pg] code.

When you insert the Center Top to Bottom code, be sure that the cursor rests at the beginning of the page before any other formatting codes. Press Alt-F3, or F11 (Reveal Codes) to verify the cursor position.

Clearing a Document

You must clear the current document from the screen before you start work on a new document—or before you retrieve a document.

Reminders

If you do not clear the current document before starting a new document, or before retrieving a document from memory, the old and the new documents will merge with one another to form a continuous (and confusing) document!

Never turn off your computer (or remove your working copy of the 5 1/4-inch WordPerfect 2 disk or the 3 1/2-inch WordPerfect 1/WordPerfect 2 (sys) disk from the disk drive) before you have cleared the current document from the screen and exited to DOS. You will know that you've returned to DOS when you see the DOS prompt (A>, B>, or C>) on your screen.

To Clear the Current Document

1. Press F7 (Exit). The following prompt appears on-screen:

   ```
   Save document? (Y/N) Yes
   ```

2. Press **Y** to begin the Save process. WordPerfect prompts:

```
Document to be saved:
```

3. Type the file name and press **Enter**. If the document already exists, WordPerfect prompts:

```
Replace (file name)? (Y/N) No
```

4. Press **Y** to save the document with the old name, or press **N** and repeat Step 3. Your document is stored under the name you select. For easy retrieval, use descriptive file names.

If you don't want to save the document you've created, or if you've saved the document previously but you want to clear your screen:

1. Press **F7** (**Exit**). The following prompt appears on-screen:

```
Save Document? (Y/N) Yes
```

2. Press **N**. The following prompt appears on-screen:

```
Exit WP? (Y/N) No
```

In response to the prompt, either press **Y** (to exit WordPerfect and return to DOS), or press **N** or **Enter** to clear the screen. If you press **F1** (**Cancel**), you will return to the document displayed on-screen.

Columns

Newspaper-Style Columns

Newspaper-style columns are read from top to bottom. The text flows from the bottom of one column to the top of the next. Newspaper-style columns are used for magazine articles, newsletters, lists, and indexes.

To define newspaper-style columns

1. Move the cursor to the position where you want columns to begin.

2. Press **Alt-F7** (**Math/Columns**). WordPerfect displays the Math/Columns menu:

   ```
   1 Math On; 2 Math Def; 3 Column
   On/Off; 4 Column Def: 0
   ```

3. Press **4** or **D** to select Column Def and display the Text Column Definition menu.

4. Press **2** or **N** to choose Number of Columns. You do not need to select 1 for Type because Newspaper is WordPerfect's default setting.

5. Enter the number of columns you want on your page (up to 24), and then press **Enter**.

6. Press **3** or **D** for Distance Between Columns. WordPerfect automatically calculates the margin settings, with 0.5" (one-half inch) between columns, but you can space your columns as close together or as far apart as you want.

In most cases, you will accept the default margin settings. If you plan to use columns of different widths, however, you must type the margin specifications.

7. To accept the default margin settings, press **Enter** or type the amount of space you want between your columns, and then press **Enter**. To enter new settings manually, press **4** or **M** to choose Margins, and then enter the new settings for Left and Right column margins. Be sure to press **Enter** after each number.

8. Press **F7** (**Exit**) to accept the settings, and press it again to exit the Text Column Definition menu.

9. Press **3** or **C** to turn on Columns.

10. Begin typing. Typing with Column on is the same as typing in a regular WordPerfect document. Your text wraps within the column until you reach the bottom of the page and then wraps to the top of the next column.

11. To turn off columns, press **Alt-F7** (**Math/Columns**), and then press **3** or **C** to choose Column On/Off and turn off columns.

After you've turned off Columns, any text you type is formatted as a normal document, and the column number disappears from the status line.

Parallel Columns

Parallel columns are read from left to right across the page. For example, parallel columns are used in a script in which names or brief instructions are typed in the first column, and the words to be spoken are typed in the second column. Inventory lists often are set up in parallel columns, as are personnel rosters and duty schedules.

You type text into parallel columns by moving from column to column across the page.

To define parallel columns

1. Press **Shift-F6** (**Center**) and type the document's heading.

2. Press **Enter** twice to space down.

3. Press **Alt-F7** (**Math/Columns**).

4. Press **4** or **D** to choose Column Def.

5. Press **1** or **T** to select Type.

6. Press **2** or **P** to select Parallel, or press **3** or **B** to select Parallel with Block Protect.

Parallel with Block Protect prevents a horizontal block of text from being split by a soft page break. When a column (other than the last column) reaches the bottom margin, the entire block of columns is moved to the next page.

If a block of columns is longer than a page, Block Protect is turned off and text continues in the same column on the next page.

7. Press **2** or **N** to choose Number of Columns.

8. Type the desired number of columns and press **Enter**.

9. Press **3** or **D** for Distance Between Columns and press **Enter**. If you want to specify a distance between columns that differs from WordPerfect's default (0.5"), enter a new specification, and press **Enter**.

10. Press **4** or **M** to choose Margins, enter margin specifications, and press **Enter**.

11. Press **F7** (**Exit**) to return to the Math/Columns menu, and then press **3** or **C** to turn on Columns.

To enter column headings

1. Press **Shift-F6** (**Center**) and type the column heading.

2. Press **Ctrl-Enter** (**Hard Page**) to move to the next column and press **Shift-F6** (**Center**).

3. Type the heading.

4. Repeat Steps 1–3 until all the column headings have been entered.

5. Press **Ctrl-Enter** (**Hard Page**) after the last column heading is typed. The cursor rests at the first column location at the left of your page.

To enter text into parallel columns

1. With the cursor positioned at the left margin, type the text for the first column.

2. When you finish typing a column entry, press **Ctrl-Enter** (**Hard Page**) and move to the next column.

3. Repeat Steps 1 and 2 for the other columns.

4. When you finish typing text under the last column heading, press **Ctrl-Enter** (**Hard Page**) to return the cursor to the left margin. You can begin typing the next group of column entries. WordPerfect automatically inserts one blank line to separate the groups of text.

To create an empty column, press **Ctrl-Enter** (**Hard Page**) twice.

Editing Columns

In Column mode, the editing keys work as explained in the following table.

The Editing Keys in Column Mode

Editing Keys	Function
Ctrl-End	Erases to the end of the line in the column being edited
Ctrl-PgDn	Erases to the end of the column starting at the cursor position

→	Moves the cursor to the right within the column
←	Moves the cursor to the left within the column
↑	Scrolls all columns
↓	Scrolls all columns
Ctrl-Home (GoTo), →	Moves the cursor to the next column
Ctrl-Home (GoTo), ←	Moves the cursor to the previous column
Home, ↓	Moves the cursor to the top of the column on the current screen
Ctrl-Home, Home, →/←	Moves the cursor to the first or last column

Comparing Documents

WordPerfect can compare the new version of a document with an old version of the document if you have saved a copy to disk under another name. Sections of the on-screen document that don't exist in the disk file are redlined. Text that exists in the disk file but not in the on-screen document is copied to the on-screen document and marked with strikeout.

To compare documents
1. Press **Alt-F5 (Mark Text)**.

```
1 Auto Ref; 2 Subdoc; 3 Index; 4
ToA Short Form; 5 Define; 6
Generate: 0
```

2. Press **6** or **G** to choose Generate.

3. Press **2** or **C** to choose Compare Screen and Disk Documents and Add Redline and Strikeout. WordPerfect displays the following prompt:

   ```
   Other Document:
   ```

4. Type the name of the file you want compare to the on-screen document.

WordPerfect compares the documents, inserting Redline and Strikeout codes. If a section of text has been moved, WordPerfect marks the affected text with Strikeout and inserts a highlighted message, THE FOLLOWING TEXT WAS MOVED, before the text, and THE PRECEDING TEXT WAS MOVED after the text.

To remove redline and strikeout

1. Press **Alt-F5** (**Mark Text**).

2. Press **6** or **G** to choose Generate.

3. Press **1** or **R** to choose Remove Redline Markings and Strikeout Text from Document. WordPerfect prompts:

   ```
   Delete redline markings and
   strikeout text? (Y/N) Yes
   ```

4. Press **Y** to remove redline and strikeout, or press **N** to leave redline and strikeout and return to the document.

5. Save your document again.

After pressing Y, all Redline codes are removed. Strikeout codes *and the text between them* are removed.

Cursor-Movement

The *cursor* is the blinking underline character that marks the location on the screen where the next character you type will appear. The cursor also marks the location in your text where codes (such as those used to create new margin settings) will be entered.

As the cursor reaches the right margin at the end of the line, WordPerfect's automatic return feature (called *word-wrap*) returns the cursor to the left margin of the next line so that you can continue typing without interruption.

You use the keys marked with arrows at the far right of the keyboard to control cursor movement. When you press an arrow key, the cursor moves in the direction indicated by the arrow on that key.

If you try to move the cursor with a cursor-arrow key on a blank screen, nothing happens. WordPerfect doesn't permit the cursor to move where nothing exists. The cursor moves only through text, spaces, or codes.

You move the cursor by pressing the arrow keys, PgUp, PgDn, +, - , or GoTo (Ctrl-Home); typing text; pressing the space bar; pressing the Tab key; or pressing the Enter key (which moves the cursor down the page along the left margin).

All keys except the function keys and the cursor-arrow keys respond much like the keys on an electric typewriter—with a few special exceptions. The Alt and Ctrl keys are used in combination with other keys to provide WordPerfect capabilities that a single key can't provide.

The Enter, or Return, key can be used as a carriage return. You also press Enter to insert blank lines in your text, such as the lines that separate paragraphs.

When the Num Lock key is activated, the cursor-movement keys become the numeric keys used to perform math functions.

Using PgDn and PgUp

Use the PgDn or PgUp keys to move the cursor a page at a time. When you press one of these keys, the prompt `Repositioning` appears on the status line.

Using GoTo

Use GoTo (Ctrl-Home) to move to a specific page or character in your document. Also use this command to move between columns, to move to the top or bottom of the page, and to move to the cursor's original position.

To move to a specific page or character

1. Check the page number on the status line.

2. Press **Ctrl-Home** (**GoTo**).

3. Type the number of the page or the character to which you want to move.

4. Press **Enter**. The cursor moves to the top of that page or to the immediate right of the first occurrence of that character.

To move between columns

1. Press **Ctrl-Home** (**GoTo**).

2. Press the left arrow to move the cursor to the previous column, or press the right arrow to move the cursor to the next column.

To move to the top or bottom of the page

1. Press **Ctrl-Home** (**GoTo**).

2. Press the up arrow to move to the top of the page,
    or press the down arrow to move to the bottom of
    the page.

To move to the cursor's original position

1. Press **Ctrl-Home** (**GoTo**).

2. Press **Ctrl-Home** (**GoTo**) again. The cursor returns
    to its original position within the document.

The cursor will return to its original position only after
you have used one of these features: Escape, GoTo,
Home and arrow keys, PgUp and PgDn, Replace, Screen
Up and Screen Down, and Search.

To move the cursor a specific number of lines or character spaces

1. Press **Esc.** The n=8 on your screen is WordPerfect's
    system default number, but you can move the
    cursor any number of lines.

2. Enter the number of lines you want to move the
    cursor.

3. Press the appropriate arrow key (up or down). The
    cursor moves in the direction indicated by the arrow
    key for exactly the number of lines you specify.

Cursor Movement Keys

The following table summarizes the cursor-movement
keys.

Cursor-Movement Keys

Horizontal Movement	*Keys*
Character left or right	← or →
Word right	Ctrl- →

Word left	Ctrl- ←
Left edge of screen	Home- ←
Right end of line	Home- →, or End
Far left of line	Home-Home- ←
Far left of line (preceding all hidden command codes)	Home-Home-Home- ←
To space following specific character	Ctrl-Home-*character*
Move text right to next tab	Tab (Normal, Insert mode on), or Indent
Jump cursor to next tab	Tab (Typeover mode)
Jump cursor to previous tab (deletes intervening text)	Shift-Tab
Move left and enter blank	Backspace (Typeover mode)
Vertical Movement	*Keys*
Line up and down	↑ and ↓
Top of screen	Home- ↑ or minus (-) on numeric keypad
Bottom of screen	Home- ↓ or plus (+) on numeric keypad
Top of current page	Ctrl-Home- ↑
End of current page	Ctrl-Home- ↓

Top of preceding page	PgUp
Top of next page	PgDn
Beginning of document	Home-Home- ↑
Beginning of document (preceding all hidden command codes)	Home-Home-Home- ↑
End of document	Home-Home- ↓
Go To page #	Ctrl-Home-#-Enter
# lines up	Esc-#- ↑
# lines down	Esc-#- ↓

Customizing WordPerfect

When you install WordPerfect, you accept the default settings for features such as margin settings, keyboard layout, cursor speed, and so on. You can use the Setup Menu (Shift-F1) to change the defaults and to customize the system to fit your work environment. When you make a change, the new setting is permanent and affects every document you create until you use the Setup menu to change the defaults again.

Setting Automatic Backups and Cursor Speed

WordPerfect's Setup menu offers two automatic backup features: Timed Backup and Original Backup. You also can change cursor speed with the Setup menu.

If you select the Timed Backup option, at specified intervals WordPerfect automatically saves the document displayed on-screen. If you have documents in both windows (Doc 1 and Doc 2), only the active document is backed up automatically.

Setting the Original Backup option causes WordPerfect to save the original file each time you replace it with an edited version. The original document is renamed with the extension .BK!. Each time you replace the document with a new version, the .BK! file is replaced with the most recently edited version.

Adjusting the Display

The Display option on the Setup menu controls many aspects of WordPerfect's screen display. For instance, you can change the color of normal text and various text attributes (if you have a color monitor), determine whether the current file name is displayed on the Status Line, select how menus and columns are shown on-screen, and so on.

You can change the following options on the Display menu:

Automatically Format and Rewrite
Colors/Fonts/Attributes
Display Document Comments
Filename on the Status Line
Graphics Screen Type
Hard Return Display Character
Menu Letter Display
Side-by-Side Columns Display

Using Fast Save

With the Fast Save option, you can save files quickly.

Reminder

With Fast Save turned on, files are saved quickly, but you cannot print fast-saved files from the disk. Instead, you must retrieve the document to the screen, then print.

To use the Fast Save option

1. Press Shift-F1 (Setup) to display the Setup menu.

2. Press 4 or F to choose Fast Save (unformatted).

3. Press Y to turn on Fast Save, or press N to turn off Fast Save.

4. Press F7 (Exit) to return to your document.

For a complete discussion of WordPerfect's customizing features, see Chapter 18 and Appendix A of Que's *Using WordPerfect 5*.

Date and Time Codes

WordPerfect can check your computer's clock and insert the current date and time in a document. It also can insert function codes that update the date and time automatically every time you retrieve the document.

Reminders

WordPerfect cannot insert the correct date and time unless your computer's clock is set correctly. Check the instruction manual for your computer to learn how to reset the clock.

To insert date codes

1. Move the cursor to the position where you want to insert the date or time code.

2. Press **Shift-F5 (Date/Outline)**. WordPerfect displays the Date/Outline menu.

3. Press **1** or **T** to choose Date Text. WordPerfect immediately types the current date, for example: July, 19, 1988. If you have set the Date/Time format to include the time, the current time is also included, for example: July 19, 1988 — 10:32 am.

Or press **2** or **C** to choose Date Code. WordPerfect types the current date and inserts a code in your document, for example: [Date:3 1, 4]. (The numbers in the code represent formatting parameters.)

Whenever you edit the document, WordPerfect automatically updates the Date Code to the current date and time.

WordPerfect can insert only one date or time code. You cannot, for example, press a key to enter the date, and then press a separate key to enter the time. You can change the date/time format so that it enters text or codes for (1) only the date, (2) only the time, or (3) both date and time.

To set the date/time format

1. Press **Shift-F5 (Date/Outline)**.

2. Press **3** or **F** to choose Date Format. WordPerfect displays the Date Format menu.

3. Enter new options, including functions to print the time of day.

4. Press **F7 (Exit)** twice to return to your document.

The Date and Time options establish the format that WordPerfect will use to print the date and time. You can mix format numbers with any text that you want to print with the date and time; for example, your prompt may include the following: Today's date is: 3 1,

4, and the time is 8:9 0. With this prompt,
WordPerfect enters the following when you use a Date/
Time code or function: Today's date is March
28, 1989, and the time is 12:47 pm.

To print just the first three characters of month and day
names, type a percent sign before the appropriate code.
For example, %3. 1, 4 (%6) displays the following: Mar.
28, 1989 (Tue).

Deleting Text

WordPerfect's design permits you to delete unwanted
text (from a single character to an entire page of
characters) and insert additional text in several ways.
Each approach works best in a specific situation.

Reminders
Remember to save your document using a name slightly
different from that of the current version before you
make major changes.

Keep in mind that the Del key is a repeat key. If you
hold it down (rather than press it once), Del deletes
multiple characters. The text that lies to the right of the
deleted characters moves in to fill the gap.

To delete a character at the cursor position
1. Use the arrow keys to position the cursor under the
   character to be deleted.

2. Press the **Del** key.

To delete a character to the left of the cursor
1. Move the cursor so that it lies one character to the
   right of the character you want to delete.

2. Press the **Backspace** key. Pressing the Backspace
   key does not delete the character above the cursor.

When you press the Backspace key, the character to the left of the cursor is erased. Any text to the right moves one character position to the left. Hold down the Backspace key to delete multiple characters to the left.

To delete a word at the cursor position

1. Position the cursor anywhere in the word to be deleted.

2. Hold down **Ctrl** while you press **Backspace**.

To delete a word to the left of the cursor

1. Place the cursor in the blank space to the right of the word to be deleted.

2. Hold down **Ctrl** while you press **Backspace**, or press **Home**, and then press **Backspace**.

To delete a word to the right of the cursor

1. Place the cursor on the first character of the word to be deleted.

2. Press **Home**, and then press the **Del** key.

To delete a line of text

1. Position the cursor where you want to begin deleting text.

2. Press **Ctrl-End** (**Delete to EOL** [End of Line]).

To delete several lines at a time

1. Count the number of lines (following the cursor) you want to erase.

2. Press **Esc**. The message n=8 appears on the status line. The default repeat value number is 8, but you can change that number to reflect the number of lines to be deleted.

3. If the number is more or less than 8, type that
    number.

4. Press **Ctrl-End** (**Delete to EOL**).

To delete a page of text

1. Position the cursor so that it lies under the character
    that begins the page of text to be deleted. (Delete to
    EOP erases text that lies between the cursor's
    position and the end of the current page.)

2. Press **Ctrl-PgDn** (**Delete to EOP** [End of Page]).
    The following prompt appears on-screen:

    ```
    Delete Remainder of page? (Y/N) No
    ```

3. Press **Y** to delete the text, or press **N** if you've
    changed your mind.

To delete blank lines

1. Move the cursor to the left margin at the beginning
    of the blank line.

2. Press **Del**. In some cases a blank line may contain a
    return code ([HRt]) and a blank space that precedes
    the word at the start of the next line. You therefore
    may have to press Del more than once to delete the
    blank characters before you reach the hidden return
    code on that line.

To delete a block of text, refer to the section on **Block
Commands**.

Document Comments

You can insert notes and reminders called *comments* in a
WordPerfect document. You can display the comments
on-screen, and you can convert the comments to text and

print them. The Document Comments feature is useful for creating text that will be reviewed by several authors.

To create a document comment

1. Press **Ctrl-F5 (Text In/Out)** to display the following menu:

   ```
   1 DOS Text; 2 Password; 3 Save
   Generic; 4 Save WP 4.2; 5 Comment:
   0
   ```

2. Press **5** or **C** to choose Comment. WordPerfect displays the Document Comment menu:

   ```
   Comment: 1 Create; 2 Edit; 3
   Convert to Text: 0
   ```

3. Press **1** or **C** to choose Create. WordPerfect places the cursor in the Document Comment editing box.

4. Type the text of your comment in the comment box. Keep your text within the lines of the box— approximately seven lines of text. You may use bold or underline in the box.

5. Press **F7 (Exit)** to return to the document.

The document comment appears on-screen in the middle of your text as a double-ruled box.

If you want to print document comments, you must convert them to text.

To change a comment to text

1. Move the cursor to a point after the comment you want to convert.

2. Press **Ctrl-F5 (Text In/Out)**.

3. Press **5** or **C** to display the Comments menu.

4. Press **3** or **T** to choose Convert to Text.

WordPerfect searches backward from the cursor and converts the first comment found. (The comment is converted whether or not it is displayed.)

To change text to a comment

1. Press **Alt-F4**, or **F12** (**Block**) and highlight the text.

2. Press **Ctrl-F5** (**Text In/Out**). WordPerfect prompts:

```
Create a comment? (Y/N) No
```

3. Press **Y** to convert the marked text to a comment.

WordPerfect places the marked text inside a comment box.

You can choose whether or not to have WordPerfect display document comments on-screen.

To turn on and off comment display

1. Press **Shift-F1** (**Setup**) to display the Setup menu.

2. Press **3** or **D** to display the Setup: Display menu.

3. Press **3** or **D** to choose Display Document Comments.

4. Press **Y** to display document comments in the text, or press **N** to hide document comments.

5. Press **F7** (**Exit**) to return to your document.

Enhancing Text

You can change the size and appearance of your text to enhance your document. Some formatting is done as you enter text simply by pressing the appropriate key, typing the text, and pressing the key again. For instance, both bold and underline are simple text enhancements that can be done anywhere in your document as you type the text. You apply some text enhancements by selecting them from the Font menu—for example, italic.

Boldfacing Text

To create boldfaced text

1. Press F6 (Bold).

2. Type the text. The text you type after pressing F6 appears brighter (or a different color) on-screen. The Pos number in the Status Line also changes in brightness or color.

3. Press F6 (Bold) again to turn off Bold.

Underlining Text

To create underlined text

1. Press F8 (Underline).

2. Type the text.

3. Press F8 (Underline) again to turn off Underline.

Changing the Base Font

WordPerfect's Font feature lets you choose among the fonts (typefaces) available for use with your printer, and also controls size, color, and certain other variations of printed text, such as outline and shadow printing, subscripts and superscripts.

When you installed your printer, you selected an *initial* font, the default base font, or the current font. (You can consider these terms interchangeable to avoid confusion.) The *base* font is the font in which text is normally printed. Other font sizes and appearance options are usually variations of the base font. If 10-point Helvetica is the base font, boldfaced text will be printed in 10-point Helvetica Bold, italics will be printed in 10-point Helvetica Italic, and so on.

The base font can be changed permanently or temporarily. Remember—to change the base font for the entire document, you must position the cursor at the beginning of your document.

To change the base font

1. Move the cursor to the point in your document where you want to change the base font.

2. Press **Ctrl-F8 (Font)** to display the following Font menu:

   ```
   1 Size; 2 Appearance; 3 Normal; 4
   Base Font; 5 Print Color: 0
   ```

3. Press **4** or **F** to select Base Font. WordPerfect displays a list of the fonts available for use with your printer.

4. Use the cursor keys to highlight the desired font.

5. Press **1** or **S** or **Enter** to select the font and return to your document.

The fonts listed are the printer's built-in fonts, plus any fonts you've selected with the Cartridges and Fonts feature.

The screen display adjusts to reflect the number of characters that can be printed in a line with the new base font in the current margin settings. If you select a 6-pitch

font, for example, the on-screen lines will be shorter
than if you select a 10-pitch font. (Pitch indicates the
number of characters per inch.)

Changing Font Attributes

Font *attributes* refer to the variations in that font's
appearance that are available with your printer for a
given base font: size, italics, boldface, shadow printing,
outline, small caps, and so on. Remember that how the
variations appear will depend on your printer.

To change font attributes

1. Press **Ctrl-F8** (**Font**).

2. Press **1** or **S** to choose Size. The following menu
    appears:

    ```
    1 Suprscpt; 2 Subscpt; 3 Fine; 4
    Small; 5 Large; 6 Vry Large; 7 Ext
    Large: 0
    ```

    Or press **2** or **A** to choose Appearance. The following
    menu appears:

    ```
    1 Bold; 2 Underln; 3 Dbl Und; 4
    Italc; 5 Outln; 6 Shadw; 7 Sm Cap;
    8 Redln; 9 Stkout: 0
    ```

3. Press the number associated with the attribute of
    your choice.

You can change an attribute of existing text by first
blocking the text with Alt-F4 or F12 and then selecting
the new attribute as described in Steps 1-3.

To restore base fonts to normal after typing your text,
press Alt-F3 or F11 (Reveal Codes). Find the attribute
codes (they appear as paired codes). Press the right-
arrow key to move the cursor past the attribute off code.

When you have made a combination of attribute changes, return the base font to normal by pressing Ctrl-F8 (Font) and pressing 3 or N for Normal. This selection cancels all size and appearance attributes.

Exiting to DOS

Even though WordPerfect's List Files feature can perform the most common DOS functions, many times it is convenient to be able to "drop out" to DOS temporarily, perform operations, and then return to your document. Use Shell (Ctrl-F1) to exit to DOS.

Reminder
If you are running WordPerfect from the WordPerfect Library shell, invoking the Shell function returns you to the Library's Shell menu.

To Exit to DOS Temporarily with Shell
1. Press **Ctrl-F1** (**Shell**). WordPerfect prompts:

   ```
   1 Go to DOS: 0
   ```

2. Press **1** or **G** to choose Go to DOS. The DOS version message displays; then another message appears:

   ```
   Enter 'EXIT' to return to
   WordPerfect
   ```

   The DOS prompt is displayed. You may now enter commands as if you had exited WordPerfect permanently.

3. To return to WordPerfect, type **exit** at the DOS prompt. The cursor returns to its position in the document before you gave the Shell command.

Exiting WordPerfect

Reminder

If you exit WordPerfect incorrectly, you may lose the
on-screen document and all the work that went into
creating it! Exiting WordPerfect incorrectly generates an
error message when you restart WordPerfect.

To Exit WordPerfect

1. Press **F7** (**Exit**), and the following message
   displays:

   ```
   Save Document? (Y/N) Yes
   ```

   The prompt provides you with one last opportunity to
   preserve your document before exiting WordPerfect. Be
   careful! If you do not save your document before you
   exit WordPerfect, you cannot retrieve it later.

2. Press **N** if you do not want to save your document,
   or press **Y** if you want to save your document, type
   the file name under which you want to save the
   document, and then press **Enter**. The following
   message appears on-screen:

   ```
   Exit WP? (Y/N) No
   ```

3. Press **Y** to exit WordPerfect and return to DOS,
   or press **N** to clear the screen and return to
   WordPerfect.

If you change your mind about exiting WordPerfect,
press **F1** (**Cancel**) to remain in WordPerfect. The
document on-screen remains unchanged.

When the DOS prompt displays, you have exited
WordPerfect. Now you can load another program or turn
off your computer.

Files

With the List Files screen, you can perform other standard DOS functions to manage your files. The options you can perform appear on the menu line of the List Files Screen. For instance, you can use this screen to copy, delete, rename, and move files. You can perform some operations on several files at a time by first *marking* the file.

Copying a File

To copy a file

1. Press **F5** (**List Files**).

2. Press **Enter** to view the list of files in the current directory; or press = (equal sign), type the path of the directory you want to view, and press **Enter**.

3. Move the highlight bar to the name of the document you want to copy; or press **N** for Name Search, begin typing the name of the document, and press **Enter**.

4. Press **8** or **C** to choose Copy. The following prompt is displayed on-screen:

   ```
   Copy this file to:
   ```

5. Type the new name and press **Enter**.

Deleting a File

To delete a file

1. Follow Steps 1-3 for copying a file.

2. Press **2** or **D** to choose Delete. The following prompt is displayed on-screen:

   ```
   Delete (filename)? (Y/N) No
   ```

3. Press **Y** to delete the file.

Renaming a File

To rename a file

1. Follow Steps 1-3 for copying a file.

2. Press **3** or **M** to select Move/Rename. The following prompt appears followed by the current name of the file:

   ```
   New name:
   ```

3. Type the new name and press **Enter**.

Moving a File

To move a file

1. Follow Steps 1-3 for copying a file.

2. Press ***** (asterisk) to mark the file.

3. Press **3** or **M** to select Move/Rename. The following prompt appears:

   ```
   Move marked files? (Y/N) No
   ```

4. Press **Y**. The following prompt appears:

   ```
   Move marked files to:
   ```

5. Type the new subdirectory name and press **Enter**.

Flush Right

Flush Right (Alt-F6) aligns the right edge of all the headings, columns, and lines of text even (flush) with the right margin. You can make text align flush right either before or after you enter the text.

To create flush right text as you type

1. Press **Alt-F6** (**Flush Right**) to move the cursor to the right margin.

2. Type your text. As you type, the cursor stays at the right margin, and the text moves to the left.

3. Press **Enter** to end Flush Right.

To align existing text with the right margin

1. Place the cursor at the left margin.

2. Press **Alt-F6** (**Flush Right**) to move the cursor and text to the right margin.

3. Press the ↓.

Footnotes and Endnotes

Footnotes and Endnotes provide a simple, standard way of referencing sources as well as offering the reader additional parenthetical information.

Footnotes are inserted at the bottom or foot of the page; *endnotes* are grouped together at the end of your document. (Some authors group endnotes at the end of each chapter or section.)

Both types of notes are marked in the text either by
numbers or by a special character such as an asterisk (*).
WordPerfect prints the footnote on the page with the text
it references.

Creating Footnotes and Endnotes

To create a footnote or an endnote

1. Move the cursor to the position where you want to
   insert a footnote or endnote number.

2. Press **Ctrl-F7** (**Footnote**) to display the Footnote/
   Endnote menu.

3. Press **1** or **F** to display the Footnote menu, or press
   2 or **E** to display the Endnote menu.

4. Press **1** or **C** to select Create. An editing screen
   appears with the cursor to the immediate right of
   the current footnote or endnote number. You can
   use all of the normal editing and function keys as
   you enter text. You can use spell-check within the
   note also.

5. Type the text.

6. Press **F7** (**Exit**) to return to your document.

WordPerfect inserts a code that includes the first 50
characters of the note. You can view the code and partial
text with Reveal Codes (Alt-F3 or F11). Use View
Document (Shift-F7, 6) to display footnotes as they will
appear when printed.

When a long footnote needs to be continued to the
following page, WordPerfect leaves one-half inch of the
note of text on the first page. If there is not enough room
to print a half-inch of the footnote and the line of text in
which the footnote number occurs, both the text and
footnote move to the next page.

Deleting Footnotes and Endnotes

Because the entire footnote (number and text) is in one code, you can delete the note in the same way you delete any other WordPerfect code.

To delete a footnote or an endnote

1. Move the cursor under the footnote or endnote you want to delete.

2. Press **Del**.

3. Press **Y** to confirm the deletion.

WordPerfect renumbers the other notes in your document automatically.

Unlike footnotes, which are printed at the bottom of the page on which you create them, endnotes are placed together, at the end of the document or where you place an Endnote Placement code. Use Ctrl-F7 (Footnote) to position an Endnote Placement code.

Generating Endnotes

To generate endnotes

1. Press **Alt-F5** (**Mark Text**).

2. Press **6** or **G** to choose Generate.

3. Press **5** or **G** to choose Generate Tables, Indexes, Automatic References, etc. WordPerfect prompts:

```
Existing tables, lists, and
  indexes will be replaced.
  Continue? (Y/N) Yes
```

4. Press **Y** to generate the endnotes.

The endnotes do not appear on-screen. Instead, WordPerfect replaces the message box with a new, boxed message:

```
Endnote Placement
```

If you want to use footnotes or endnotes, but don't like the format WordPerfect has chosen for them, you can use Ctrl-F7 to change the numbering style, placement, and format.

Forms

WordPerfect documents are formatted for a particular size and type of paper. This formatting information is saved with the document in the form of a default Paper Size/Type specification or a special Paper Size/Type code that you enter in the document.

When you choose a form using the Paper Size/Type menu, WordPerfect displays the forms you've designed, as well as the default form types supplied with the program. WordPerfect matches the forms from this Paper Type menu with the forms you define in the Form Type menu. If the program can't find a corresponding definition, it chooses the form it considers to be the closest match.

WordPerfect comes with a list of default form sizes and types, and you also can add customized form definitions to meet your special needs.

You can change the following options when defining or editing a form type:

>   *Form Size*
>   *Orientation*
>   *Initially Present*
>   *Location*
>   *Page Offsets*

Function Keys

The keys labeled F1 to F10 on the left of the keyboard
(or F1 to F12 at the top of the IBM Enhanced Keyboard)
are *function keys*. Each function key can carry out four
tasks when used by itself or in combination with another
key.

You routinely use the function keys to give your
computer instructions called *commands*.

The function keys are assigned as follows:

Function Keys

Name	*Key(s)*
Block	Alt-F4
Bold	F6
Cancel	F1
Center	Shift-F6
Date/Outline	Shift-F5
Exit	F7
Flush Right	Alt-F6
Font	Ctrl-F8
Footnote	Ctrl-F7
Format	Shift-F8
Help	F3
→ Indent	F4
→ Indent ←	Shift-F4
List Files	F5
Macro	Alt-F10
Macro Def	Ctrl-F10
Mark Text	Alt-F5
Math/Columns	Alt-F7
Merge Codes	Shift-F9
Merge R	F9
Merge/Sort	Ctrl-F9
Move	Ctrl-F4

Print	Shift-F7
Replace	Alt-F2
Retrieve Document	Shift-F10
Reveal Codes	Alt-F3
Save	F10
Screen	Ctrl-F3
→ Search	F2
← Search	Shift-F2
Shell	Ctrl-F1
Spell	Ctrl-F2
Style	Alt-F8
Switch	Ctrl-F8
Tab Align	Shift-F3
Text In/Out	Ctrl-F6
Thesaurus	Ctrl-F5
Underline	Alt-F1
	F8

Some function keys are used as toggle switches to turn a feature on and off. For example, to create boldface type, you first press function key F6 (to turn on Bold); then, you type the text that will be printed in boldface type, and press F6 again to turn off Bold.

Some function keys permit you to select from a menu. When you press Ctrl-F7, for example, your system displays the Footnote/Endnote menu.

Some function keys start a feature that is ended by pressing the Enter key. For instance, you activate the Center feature by pressing Shift-F6, and end centering by pressing Enter (or the ↓ key).

Graphics

With the Graphics feature you can enhance the appearance of your document with graphics boxes and lines.

Defining Graphics Boxes

You can use four types of boxes: figure, table, text box, and user-defined box. In the boxes, you can insert text; graphics from the Fonts/Graphics disk; or graphics, charts, and graphs created in other external programs. Or you can create an empty box. Graphics boxes can be placed in the body of a document, in headers, in footers, and in endnotes. When you create a box, you specify its contents, its caption, its type, its placement on the page, and its size.

To Create a Graphics Box

1. Move the cursor to the point in your document where you want the graphic image to appear.

2. Press **Alt-F9** (**Graphics**).

3. Select a box type.

When you choose a box type, a menu appears. The name differs depending on the type of box you select; for example, if you select table, WordPerfect displays the following menu:

```
Table: 1 Create; 2 Edit; 3 new
   Number; 4 Options: 0
```

4. Press **1** or **C** to select Create.

The Table: Definition menu appears. (Again, the name of the menu differs depending on the type of box you are creating.)

5. Select the options you want to specify.

6. Enter the changes.

7. Press **F7** to return to your document.

Only an outline appears on-screen after you create a box. To see how the document will appear when printed, use View Document (Shift-F7, 6).

Creating Graphics Lines

With WordPerfect, you can create vertical and horizontal lines on the printed page. The lines can be shaded or black.

To Create Graphics Lines

1. Press **Alt-F9** (**Graphics**).

2. Press **5** or **L** to select Line.

3. Press **1** or **H** to select Horizontal Line, or press **2** or **V** to select Vertical Line. WordPerfect displays the Horizontal Line menu or the Vertical Line menu.

4. Choose an option and enter the appropriate information.

5. Press **F7** (**Exit**) to return to the editing screen.

A graphics line can't be edited, but it can be deleted (by deleting the hidden function codes) and replaced with a new line. To see how a line will print, use View Document (Shift-F7, 6 or V).

Headers/Footers

A *header* is information (text, numbers, or graphics) that prints automatically at the margin at the top of the page. A *footer* is information printed automatically at the margin at the bottom of the page. Typical header and footer information may include chapter titles, page numbers, dates, and similar information.

To see headers or footers on-screen, use either View Document (Shift-F7, 6) or Reveal Codes (Alt-F3, or F11).

To create a header or footer

1. Press **Shift-F8 (Format)** to display the Format menu.

2. Press **2** or **P** to display the Format: Page menu.

3. Press **3** or **H** to select Headers, or press **4** or **F** to select Footers. You can create two headers (A and B) and two footers (A and B). The following prompt appears:

   ```
   1 Header A; 2 Header B: 0
   ```

   Or

   ```
   1 Footer A; 2 Footer B: 0
   ```

4. Press **1** or **A**, or **2** or **B**. WordPerfect displays the following menu:

   ```
   1 Discontinue; 2 Every Page; 3 Odd
     Pages; 4 Even Pages; 5 Edit: 0
   ```

5. Press **2** or **P** if you want the header (or footer) to appear on every page.

Or press **3** or **O** if you want the header (or footer) to appear on odd pages only.

Or press **4** or **V** if you want the header (or footer) to appear on even pages only.

6. Type the header (or footer) text using any of WordPerfect's formatting features.

7. Press **F7 (Exit)** twice to return to your document.

You can make changes to a header or footer from anywhere in a document. For instance, you can change the text or the appearance of the text in your footer.

To make changes, select Edit from the Header or Footer menu. In addition to including and formatting text, you can add automatic page numbering to a header or footer by including ^B (Ctrl-B) in the header or footer. For example, you can specify the footer to read it and be numbered consecutively.

To include automatic page numbering in headers and footers

1. Type any text that will precede the page number.

2. Press **Ctrl-B**.

3. Press **F7** (**Exit**).

Help

WordPerfect has an on-line Help feature that you can access while working on WordPerfect documents. If you have a question about what a particular function key does, just press the Help key (F3) to display information about that function key. In addition to the function keys, the Help screens also explain the Esc, Del, Ins, Backspace, Tab, Home, and cursor-arrow keys.

To access Help

1. Press **F3** (**Help**) to display the Help screen.

2. Press the key about which you want to know more.

For example, if you press **Shift-F7** (**Print**), the Print Help menu is displayed. From within the Print Help screen, you can learn more about Printer Control by pressing 4 or C.

After you have reviewed the Help information, return to your file by pressing **Enter** or the **space bar**.

Note

Press F3 (Help) twice to display the keyboard template. After accessing Help, type any letter of the alphabet to view a list of the features that begin with that letter.

Hyphenating Words

When a line of text becomes too long to fit within the margins, the last word wraps to the next line. With short words, wrapping doesn't present much of a problem. With long words, two problems can occur: (1) if justification is off, large gaps can appear at the right margin producing a document composed of very ragged text; (2) if justification is on, large spaces between words become visually distracting.

Hyphenating the word at the end of the line solves these formatting problems. When you use WordPerfect's hyphenation feature, the program fits as much of the word as possible on the line, hyphenates the word, and wraps the rest of the word to the next line. To control hyphenation, use one of three possible settings: off, manual, or automatic.

When you use manual hyphenation, WordPerfect prompts you to position the hyphen in a word that needs to be broken.

If you set hyphenation to Auto, WordPerfect uses an internal set of rules to hyphenate common words. Because many words are not covered by these rules, WordPerfect prompts you for the proper hyphenation of these words just as if you'd selected Manual hyphenation.

To turn on hyphenation

1. Press **Shift-F8 (Format)** to display the Format menu.

2. Press **1** or **L** to display the Format: Line menu.

3. Press **1** or **Y** for Hyphenation. The Hyphenation menu is displayed at the bottom of the screen:

   ```
   1 Off; 2 Manual; 3 Auto: 0
   ```

4. Press **2** or **M** for Manual, or press **3** or **A** for Auto.

5. Press **F7 (Exit)**.

A [Hyph on] code is inserted in the text. Hyphenation remains on until you turn it off. To turn off hyphenation, follow Steps 1-3; select **1** or **F** for Step 4.

As you type or scroll through your document, WordPerfect automatically hyphenates words if you selected Auto. If you selected Manual, or if WordPerfect can't find a rule to hyphenate the word, the program calls your attention to words that should be hyphenated. When it reaches a word, such as "justification," WordPerfect beeps and displays a message similar to the following:

```
Position hyphen; Press ESC
  justifi-cation
```

To select hyphenation

Use the cursor keys to move the hyphen to another hyphenation point; then press **Esc**. Or press **F1 (Cancel)** if you don't want to hyphenate the word. If you don't hyphenate the word, it wraps to the next line and a Cancel Hyphenation code [/] is inserted before the word. You must delete the code manually if you decide to hyphenate the word.

At first glance, a hyphen looks simply like a hyphen, but WordPerfect uses, and permits you to use several kinds of hyphens.

A *hard hyphen* is part of the spelling of a word, as in *father-in-law* and *jack-of-all-trades*. A hard hyphen is displayed and printed at all times. The hard hyphen code appears on the Reveal Codes screen as [—]. If a hard hyphen appears in a word that needs to be hyphenated, WordPerfect uses the hard hyphen as the breaking point instead of prompting you for a hyphenation decision. To enter a hard hyphen, press the Hyphen key (located on the same key as the underline character).

The *hyphen character* appears the same on-screen as a hard hyphen. WordPerfect treats the hyphen character as if it were a character; the word containing a hard hyphen is not split at the hard hyphen when it falls within the hyphenation zone. In on-screen and in Reveal Codes, the hyphen appears as an unhighlighted —. To enter a hyphen character, press Home, Hyphen. Be sure to use the Hyphen key in the numeric key row, not the minus sign on the numeric keypad.

A *soft hyphen* is inserted between syllables during hyphenation. Soft hyphens are visible and print only when they appear as the last character in a line; otherwise, they remain hidden. Soft hyphens appear in Reveal Codes as a highlighted —. You can insert soft hyphens at points where you want hyphenation to occur by pressing Ctrl-Hyphen.

An *invisible soft return* character is entered by WordPerfect when hyphenation is turned off and a long word extends from the left margin beyond the right margin. (The invisible soft return is not the same as the normal [SRt] soft return inserted at the end of a line by WordPerfect's word wrap feature.)

The invisible soft return is useful for preventing empty spaces in lines caused by words separated by slashes, which WordPerfect normally treats as single, long words. To make expressions such as and/or, either/or or words connected with an ellipsis divide properly, press Home, Enter to insert an invisible soft return.

To insert a *dash* in your text, use a combination of two kinds of hyphens. For the first hyphen, press Home, Hyphen for the hyphen character. For the second hyphen, press Hyphen for a hard hyphen. WordPerfect will not separate the two hyphens at the end of a line.

When you want to keep two or more words together, for instance *San Francisco*, insert a *hard space* between the words by pressing Home, space bar. Hard spaces signal WordPerfect to treat the words as a character string: WordPerfect will not divide the string when it falls at the end of a line but will move the entire word group to the following line. A hard space appears as [—] in Reveal Codes.

Always use Reveal Codes (Alt-F3 or F11) to delete unwanted hard and soft hyphens.

The Hyphenation Zone

WordPerfect decides which words to hyphenate by using a hyphenation zone. When hyphenation is on, the zone determines whether a word should be hyphenated or wrapped to the next line. The hyphenation zone is preset in percentages of line length: the left hyphenation zone is preset at 10%; the right hyphenation zone is set at 4%.

When hyphenation is turned on, three things can happen to words that fall near the right margin:

1. Words that start on or after the left hyphenation zone but do not reach the right margin remain in position.

2. Words that begin on or after the left hyphenation zone and pass the right margin wrap to the next line.

3. Words that start before the left hyphenation zone and pass over the right hyphenation zone require hyphenation.

The distance between the left and right hyphenation zones determines the size of words selected for hyphenation. The shorter the distance between the two zones, the more hyphenation is needed. You can use Shift-F8 (Format) to temporarily change the hyphenation zone.

Indenting

Although WordPerfect's Tab and Indent features are similar, they each have specific uses.

Tab	Indents only the first line of the paragraph from the left margin
F4 (Indent)	Indents the entire paragraph from the left margin
Shift-F4	Indents the entire paragraph from both (Left-Right margins Indent)

Use Indent (F4) to indent an entire paragraph from the left margin. When you press F4 the cursor moves one tab stop to the right, and the left margin is reset temporarily. Everything you type, until you press Enter, is indented one tab stop. To indent more than one tab stop, press F4 until the cursor rests at the point where you want to begin.

Use Left-Right Indent (Shift-F4) to indent a paragraph from both the right and left margins. When you press Shift-F4, the cursor moves to the right one tab stop and temporarily resets both the left and right margins. Everything you type, until you press Enter, is indented one tab stop from the left margin and the same distance from the right margin. To indent more than one tab stop from both margins, press Shift-F4 more than once.

To indent text from the left margin as you type

1. Move the cursor to the left margin.

2. Press **F4** (**Indent**). The cursor moves to the next tab setting.

3. Type your text.

4. Press **Enter** to end indenting.

The text that you type now begins at the original left margin.

To indent text from both margins as you type

1. Press **Shift-F4** (**Left-Right Indent**).

2. Type your text.

3. Press **Enter** to end indenting and return to the original margin settings.

To indent an existing paragraph

1. Move the cursor to the first character of the text you want to indent (or to the left of a tab indent at the beginning of a paragraph).

2. Press **F4** (**Indent**) or **Shift-F4** (**Left-Right Indent**).

3. Press the ↓ to redraw the screen so that the entire paragraph is indented.

A *hanging paragraph* is formed so that the first line is flush with the left margin and the rest of the paragraph is indented to the first tab stop.

To create a hanging paragraph

1. Move the cursor to the left margin.

2. Press **F4** (**Indent**) to move the cursor to the next tab stop.

3. Press **Shift-Tab** (**Margin Release**). The cursor moves back to its original position, at the left margin.

4. Type your text.

5. Press **Enter** to end the hanging paragraph.

Caution

Never use the space bar for indenting or tabbing. If your printer supports proportional spacing, text will not align properly at the left indent or tab stop. Instead, use the Tab or Indent keys.

Indexing

WordPerfect's indexing feature creates an alphabetized list of index headings and subheadings (called *entries*) for a document. To create an index, you use **Alt-F5** (**Mark Text**) to *mark* or specify the words you want to include in the index, then you define an index format, and finally you generate the index.

You can issue the command to generate a table of contents or list from anywhere in a document, but an index *must* be generated with the cursor at the end of the document.

Caution

An [EndDef] code is inserted at the end of the index. If
you edit the document after generating the index, be
aware that any text you enter between the [DefMark]
and [EndDef] codes will be deleted if you generate a
new index. To prevent this from happening, delete the
[EndDef] code *before* you generate the new index.

Justification

WordPerfect's Right-justification feature causes spaces
to be inserted between words and letters so that the text
aligns flush with the right margin. Text that is not
justified has a ragged right margin. You cannot see
right-justification on-screen. When you print your
document with a printer capable of proportional spacing,
the text prints even with the right margin. The default
for right-justification is on.

To turn off justification temporarily

1. Press **Ctrl-F8** (**Format**) to display the Format
   menu.

2. Press **1** or **L** to display the Format: Line menu.

3. Press **3** or **J** to select Justification.

4. Press **N** to turn off justification.

5. Press **F7** (**Exit**) to return to your document.

Line Spacing

To format your text, you can change both the line
spacing and the line height.

WordPerfect's line spacing default is single-spacing. To double-space or triple-space a document, you can change the line-spacing default rather than enter hard returns as you type. Line-spacing changes can be made permanently or temporarily. You won't see changes in line spacing on-screen except when you select single (1), double (2), or triple (3) line spacing.

To temporarily change line spacing

1. Press **Shift-F8** (Format) to display the Format menu.

2. Press **1** or **L** to display the Format: Line menu.

3. Press **6** or **S** to select Line Spacing.

4. Type the amount of line spacing you want (with up to two decimal places) and press **Enter**. For example, to double-space, type 2. For one and one-half spaces, type 1.5.

5. Press **F7** (Exit) to return to your document.

The vertical distance between the base of a line of text and the base of the line of text above or below is called *line height*. WordPerfect 5 automatically controls line height. If the line height was not adjusted and you changed to a larger type size, the vertical spacing would appear very cramped on the printed page.

Because WordPerfect handles line-height changes automatically, you usually don't need to adjust it manually except for special circumstances. If, for example, your document is one page plus two lines and you want the text to fit on one page, you could change the line height to accommodate the extra lines.

Use **Shift-F8** (Format) to change line height.

Lists

If your document contains figures, illustrations, tables, maps, and other illustrations, you may want to list these resources in a reference table. Usually a list appears on a page by itself following the table of contents.

As with tables of contents, creating a list requires that you use **Alt-F5** (**Mark Text**) to mark the text for the list, define the list, and generate the list.

You can create up to nine lists per document.

Locking Documents

You can *lock* your document so that no one (not even you) will be able to retrieve or print it without the password. Other files associated with the document, such as backup files, undelete files, and move files, also are locked.

Reminder

If you forget a password, WordPerfect's technical support staff can do nothing to help. The document is unavailable forever.

To save your file as a locked document

1. Press **Ctrl-F5** (**Text In/Out**).

2. Press **2** or **P** to select Password.

3. Press **1** or **A** to select Add.

4. Type the password and press **Enter.** The password can be up to 23 characters long. WordPerfect prompts:

   ```
   Re-Enter Password:
   ```

5. Type the password again and press **Enter**.

Every time you retrieve the document, WordPerfect asks you for the password. To unlock a document, follow Steps 1-2. For Step 3, press 2 or R to select Remove.

Macros

A macro is a file you create to represent a series of keystrokes. Macros automate time-consuming and tedious tasks such as typing **Sincerely** every time you write a business letter. After you set up a macro, you can use it to do, almost instantly, what would otherwise require many keystrokes.

Creating Macros

To Record Macro Keystrokes

1. Press **Ctrl-F10 (Macro Define)** to turn on the macro definition recorder. The following prompt appears in the lower left corner of your screen:

```
Define macro:
```

This prompt is asking for the name of your macro. WordPerfect has three ways to name a macro when the Define Macro: prompt is displayed:

Alt-letter macro. To assign an Alt-*letter* combination to a macro, press and hold the Alt key while you type a letter between A and Z. Use Alt-*letter* names for macros you want to save and use again.

Enter macro. To create a temporary macro that you will use only until you create another temporary macro, do not type a name; just press Enter. WordPerfect names the macro.

Named macro. To name a macro, type a descriptive one-
to eight-character name and press Enter.

2. Type the macro name and press **Enter**; or, for a
    temporary macro, just press **Enter**. WordPerfect
    prompts:

    ```
    Description:
    ```

3. Enter a description of up to 39 characters that tells
    what the macro does; or, for a temporary macro,
    skip this step. WordPerfect does not prompt you to
    enter a description.

4. Press **Enter** to begin recording keystrokes. For a
    temporary macro, skip this step.

The Macro Def prompt blinks in the lower left of the
screen. Think of this blinking message as a reminder
that the program is recording and remembering your
keystrokes.

5. Type the keystrokes (commands and/or text) that
    you want to record in the macro file. Type the
    keystrokes in the exact order that you want them
    played back when you run the macro.

6. Press **Ctrl-F10** (**Macro Define**) to end macro
    definition.

WordPerfect now saves the macro in a permanent disk
file and returns you to the document screen.

Running Macros

The way you run (play back) a macro depends on the
method you used to name the macro.

Reminder

Keep in mind that you can stop a macro while it is
running by pressing F1 (Cancel). A macro stops
automatically if it encounters an error message or if it
contains a Search or Replace function and cannot locate
the search text.

To run an Alt-letter macro

Hold down the Alt key while you type the letter
assigned to the macro—for example, Alt-B.

To run a named macro

1. Press Alt-F10 (Macro).

2. Type the name of the macro you want to run.

3. Press Enter.

To run a temporary Enter key macro

1. Press Alt-F10 (Macro).

2. Press Enter.

Margins, Left and Right

WordPerfect presets all initial or default settings for
margins, tabs, and other basic features. If these settings
do not fit your needs, you either can change the settings
(temporarily) for the document on which you are
working, or you can change the settings permanently
with the Setup menu (Shift-F1).

WordPerfect's default margins are one inch for the left
and one inch for the right—appropriate margins for
8 1/2 by 11-inch paper. Unlike WordPerfect 4.2,
WordPerfect 5 measures margins from the right and left
edges of the paper, or from the perforation for pin-feed
paper.

If you want to change the margins, simply measure your stationery or paper and decide how many inches of white space you want as margins. Because measuring in rows and columns can be confusing, set margins in inches.

New margin settings override previous settings. You can change margins in the middle of a line, but WordPerfect will enter a hard return [HRt] before the new margin code to ensure that the current line is formatted with the existing margins and that text that follows the code is formatted with the new margins.

To change the margin settings

1. Place the cursor at the left margin of the line where you want the new margin setting to begin.

2. Press **Shift-F8 (Format)** to display the Format menu.

3. Press **1** or **L** to display the Format: Line menu.

If you change your mind about the new margin settings, pressing F1 (Cancel) won't cancel the new margin settings; you must use Reveal Codes (Alt-F3, or F11) to remove the [L/R Mar:1",1"] code.

If you always use different margins than the default, you can permanently change the margins for all future documents.

To change the left and right margins permanently

1. Press **Shift-F1 (Setup)**.

2. Press **5** or **I** to display the Initial Settings menu.

3. Press **4** or **I** for Initial Codes.

4. Press **Shift-F8 (Format)**.

5. Press **1** or **L** to display the Format: Line menu.

6. Press **7** or **M** to select Margins (Left/Right).

7. Type a new value for the left margin and press **Enter**.

8. Type a new value for the right margin and press **Enter**.

9. Press **F7** (**Exit**) three times to return to your document.

To change top and bottom margins, see the section "Positioning Text on a Page."

Master Documents

Use the Master Document feature to manage large projects by following this procedure:

Maintain and store sections of a long document as individual files called *subdocuments*.

Build a skeleton or *master document* that includes references to each subdocument.

Temporarily *expand* the master document to link all the individual files (to generate a table of contents for example).

Separate or *condense* the expanded document into its component parts (subdocuments).

A master document file consists of two kinds of files: master document files and subdocument files. The master document file is a regular WordPerfect file which contains codes that reference the subdocument files. In addition to the codes, the master document file can contain anything else you want to include (like the table of contents). The subdocument contains the text for each section of the total document. You can include as many subdocuments as you need.

Math

WordPerfect's Math feature is designed to provide limited calculation capabilities for simple math operations, like preparing an invoice or developing a sales report.

Vertical Column Calculation

WordPerfect allows you to calculate and display the totals of numbers in columns, using the following procedure:

To calculate in vertical columns

1. Set the tabs for your columns.

2. Define the type and format of your columns.

3. Turn on Math, using **Alt-F7** (**Math/Columns**).

4. Enter caption text, numbers, and math operators in the columns.

5. Calculate the results.

6. Turn off Math.

You enter both the numbers for your columns and math operators to perform calculations. You can use as many as six Math operators in a Math numeric column, as shown in the following table.

WordPerfect Math Operators

Hier. Level	Oper.	Name	Function
2	+	Subtotal	Add all numbers in the column above the + sign (from the last total or subtotal taken or from the beginning of the column).
2	t	Extra Subtotal	Treat the number immediately following this operator as a subtotal.
3	=	Total	Add all subtotals (+) and extra subtotals (t) since the last total
3	T	Extra total	Treat the number immediately following this operator as a total.
4	*	Grand total	Add all totals (=) and extra totals (T) since the last Grand total.
1,2,3	N	Negate	Reverse the sign of the result or number immediately following this operator for use in further calculations.

Math operators are symbols that tell WordPerfect both the type of calculation you want to perform, and where the result will be displayed. You enter a Math operator by using the Tab key to position the cursor at the location where the results should be displayed, and then entering the appropriate operator.

When you enter an operator, only the operator is
displayed (the math results are not shown until you
invoke the Calculate function).

Horizontal Calculations

Numeric and total columns calculate vertical addition of
numbers. You can use **Alt-F7** (**Math/Columns**) to
calculate another type of Math column—the calculation
(0) column. Calculation columns calculate numbers
within the same line of a WordPerfect document and are
also called horizontal calculations.

When you enter 0 for the column type code,
WordPerfect automatically moves the cursor down to
the middle of the screen to allow you to enter a formula
for the calculation column.

Formulas are composed of numbers, column identifiers,
and math operators. *Do not use spaces in calculation
formulas.* Your formulas can include the following four
standard arithmetic operators:

    +   Add
    -    Subtract
    *   Multiply
    /   Divide

The formula is calculated from left to right. If you want
a math term to calculate before other items, enclose that
term in parentheses. Unlike algebra, however, you
cannot use nested parentheses, as in: (3+(3*A))-B. If
you want to use a fraction in an equation, place it in
parentheses or use its decimal equivalent: (1/3), .33.

Merge

Merge inserts variable data into a fixed format. With WordPerfect's Merge feature, you can create personalized form letters from an address list, produce phone lists, print labels, piece together complicated reports, or fill in forms.

Assembling Documents with Merge

WordPerfect uses just two documents to perform a merge:

The *primary (document) file* holds a skeleton document into which pieces of data are merged. Most of the primary file remains constant. The primary file contains two elements: the fixed text and the merge codes, which are implanted where the variable items will be added to the fixed text.

The *secondary (data) file* contains the data, or variable information, that is merged into the primary file. Information in the secondary file is organized like information on filing cards. The information on one filing card (or one secondary file entry) is known as a *record*. Records are divided into *fields*. For example, mailing list fields usually consist of the first name, last name, company name, street address, city, state, and ZIP.

Creating the secondary file—the data file—is usually the first step in the merge procedure.

Reminders

Remember that a secondary file consists of records (ending with ^E), which have a number of fields (ending with ^R). The structure must be uniform; otherwise, the merge won't work properly.

Keep in mind that every data record must have the same number of fields.

The fields in all records must be in the same order. For example, if the first name is in field 1, but one record has the last name in field 1, WordPerfect will print a last name where the first name should be.

To Create a Sample Secondary File

1. Clear the screen and place the cursor at the top left margin.

2. Type a name and address, pressing **F9** (**Merge**) at the end of the each line (field). When you press Merge R, WordPerfect inserts a ^R code and a hard return [HRt] code.

3. At the end of the last line of the record, press **Shift-F9** (**Merge Codes**) after you press **F9** (**Merge R**).

4. Press **E** to enter a ^E code that marks the end of the record. WordPerfect enters a ^E code and a hidden Hard Page [HPg] code.

5. Enter the next record.

6. When you finish entering data, save the file under a name that indicates its purpose: for example, LETTERS.DAT or NAMES.MRG.

Creating Primary Files

A primary file contains fixed text and special merge codes. The codes guide WordPerfect to bring in specific records from your secondary merge file and these records where the codes are implanted. The most common code is the field number code ^Fn^. The n indicates a field number (or name) of each record in the secondary file.

To Create a Sample Primary File

1. Begin typing a sample letter. When you get to the line where you want the addressee's name entered, press **Shift-F9** (**Merge Codes**). WordPerfect displays the Merge Codes menu:

```
^C; ^D; ^E; ^F; ^G; ^N; ^O; ^P;
  ^Q; ^S; ^T; ^U; ^V:
```

For an explanation of these codes, see the following table.

Merge Codes

Code	*Function*
^C	To temporarily halt a merge in order to display a message or to allow any entry from the keyboard
^D	To insert the current date into the merge document
^E	To mark the end of a secondary file record
^F*n*^	To indicate a field name or number in a primary file
^G	To activate a macro
^N	To look for the next record to continue the merge in progress (for a primary file)
^P	To activate a primary file
^Q	To quit (terminate) a merge
^R	To mark the end of a field in a secondary file
^S	To activate a secondary file

^T   To send to the printer the merged text

^U   To update (rewrite or view) the screen
          displaying the merge in progress

^V   To transfer merge codes to a document
          created by a merge

2. Press **F**. WordPerfect prompts:

```
Field:
```

3. Press the number of the current field (**1**, in this
   case), and then press **Enter**, because you want field
   1 (name, for example) from the secondary file to be
   printed here. WordPerfect inserts an ^F1^ code in
   your document at the cursor.

4. Repeat Steps 1–3 for field 2 (company), field 3
   (address), field 4 (city), and field 5 (salutation).

5. When you finish typing the letter, save it with a
   name that indicates its purpose: for example,
   LETTER.MRG or MERGE.LET.

Your primary file will now show the information
merged from the secondary file.

Running a Merge

The codes ^F1^, ^F2^, ^F3^, and so on, instruct
WordPerfect to reach into the secondary (data) file, copy
the appropriate fields, and insert them into the letter. For
instance, WordPerfect inserts field 1 at ^F1^, field 2 at
^F2^, and so on.

To merge primary and secondary files

1. Press **Ctrl-F9** (**Merge/Sort**). WordPerfect displays the Merge/Sort menu:

   ```
   1 Merge; 2 Sort; 3 Sort Order: 0
   ```

2. Press **1** or **M** to select Merge. WordPerfect prompts:

   ```
   Primary file:
   ```

3. Type the name of the primary (document) file in which you saved the letter, and then press **Enter**. WordPerfect prompts:

   ```
   Secondary file:
   ```

4. Type the name of the secondary (data) file in which you saved the address data, and then press **Enter**.

The two files are merged, and the resulting merge-printed letters are displayed on the screen. You can edit them now or save them in a file.

To merge directly to the printer

1. In the primary file (the letter), use **Merge Codes** (**Shift- F9**) to enter the following codes at the end of the letter (you must press **Shift-F9** once for each code): ^T^N^P^P. The following table shows what the codes do.

Codes for Sending a Merge to the Printer

Code	Function
^T	Sends to the printer all text that has been merged so far

^N   Moves to the next record (name and
                  address) in the secondary file

^P*filename*^P   Starts the merge again, using the
                  file name indicated. If no file name
                  is entered between the ^P codes, the
                  same primary file is used again.

2. Save the letter.

3. Turn on the printer.

4. Press **Ctrl-F9** (Merge/Sort) to start the merge
   operation.

5. Press **1** or **M** to choose Merge.

6. Type the primary file name and press **Enter**.

7. Type the secondary file name and press **Enter**.

WordPerfect prints your letters.

Creating Labels

You can use Merge to print labels on various kinds of
label stock. Creating a primary file that matches the size
of your labels is a straightforward process, but you will
need to enter special formatting codes to tell
WordPerfect and your printer where to place the label
data when you merge print.

Reminder

First create a secondary (address) file. Then you can use
that file to print mailing labels.

To Create the Primary Label File

1. Press **Shift-F8** (Format) to display the Format
   menu.

2. Press 2 or P to choose Page.

3. Press 5 or M to choose Margins, Top and Bottom.

4. Type 0 for the Top margin, and then press Enter.

5. Type 0 for the Bottom margin, and then press Enter twice to return to the Format menu.

6. Press 1 or L to choose Line.

7. Press 7 or M to choose Margins, Left and Right.

8. Enter values for left and right label margins. You may have to experiment to find the right settings for your printer. Try .5" for the left margin and 0" for the right margin.

9. Press Enter twice to return to the Format menu.

10. Press 4 or O to choose Other.

11. Press 1 or A to choose Advance.

12. Press 2 or D to choose Down. WordPerfect prompts:

    ```
    Adv. down 0"
    ```

13. Type .25" to advance the printhead down to the first line of the first label. You may have to experiment to find the proper Advance measurement for your printer.

You now need to set the paper size for printing on label stock.

14. Press Enter twice to return to the Format menu.

15. Press 2 or P to choose Page.

16. Press 8 or S to choose Paper Size/Type.

17. At the Paper Size menu, press **0** or **O** to choose Other.

18. At the Width: and Height: prompts, type the dimensions of the label stock you will use, and then press **Enter**.

19. At the Paper Type menu, press **4** or **L** to choose Labels. WordPerfect displays the Format Page menu. If no special label type is in the driver supplied for your printer, WordPerfect inserts an asterisk (*) at the Paper Type prompt.

20. Press **Enter** to return to the Format menu.

21. Press **Home, Home, Home,** ↓ to move the cursor past any hidden codes in the file.

22. Enter ^F*n*^ codes for the fields you want printed on your labels. (See the preceding instructions for formatting primary files.)

23. Save the file under a descriptive name.

24. Press **F7** (**Exit**) and press **N** twice to clear the screen.

25. Merge-print the primary (label) file with your secondary merge file.

Numbering Lines

WordPerfect can number the lines in your document. With line numbering, you can easily refer to a particular clause in a legal document or to a specific passage in a manuscript. For instance, you can refer to page 11, line 26 to cite a passage.

When you begin Line Numbering, WordPerfect inserts a [Ln Num:On] code in your document and begins numbering that line at 1. Numbers are not displayed on-screen; they appear when you print the document or use View Document (Shift-F7, 6).

To Number Lines Automatically

1. Move the cursor to the position where you want line numbering to begin (usually at the beginning of your document).

2. Press **Shift-F8 (Format)** to display the Format menu.

3. Press **1** or **L** to display the Format: Line menu.

4. Press **5** or **N** to select Line Numbering.

5. Press **Y** to turn on Line Numbering and display the Format: Line Numbering menu.

6. Press **Enter** to accept the default settings; or select the option you want to change, enter the desired information, and then press **F7 (Exit)** to return to the editing screen.

To turn off Line Numbering, repeat Steps 1–4. In Step 5, press N.

When you turn on Line Numbering, you can change how the lines are numbered with the following options:

Count Blank Lines
Number Every n Lines
Position of Number from Left Edge
Starting Number
Restart Number on Each Page

Numbering Pages

Automatic page numbering is as easy as telling
WordPerfect how and where you want the numbers to
appear on the page. Numbering begins with whatever
number you select. Be sure to place the cursor at the
beginning of your document if you want page
numbering to begin on the first page.

You can select any one of three basic page number
positions: (1) top of the page (left, right, or center); (2)
bottom of the page (left, right, or center); or (3) facing
pages (at the left side of even pages, or at the right side
of odd pages).

To select page number position

1. Press **Shift-F8** (**Format**) to display the Format
    menu.

2. Press **2** or **P** to display the Format: Page menu.

3. Press **7** or **P** to display the Format: Page Numbering
    menu.

4. Type the number that corresponds to the position
    where you want page numbers to appear.

5. Press **F7** (**Exit**) to return to your document.

Page numbers are aligned with the left and right
margins. WordPerfect positions page numbers at the top
or bottom page margin and leaves a space between the
page number and the body text equivalent to the line
height of the page number font plus 1/6 of an inch. You
can change page numbering at any point in your
document, and the change takes effect from that point
forward.

To change the starting page number

1. Move the cursor to the top of the page where you want to start numbering.

2. Press **Shift-F8** (**Format**) to display the Format menu.

3. Press **2** or **P** to display the Format: Page menu.

4. Press **6** or **N** to select New Page Number.

5. Type the new page number and press **Enter**.

6. Press **F7** (**Exit**) to return to your document.

If you turn on page numbering and later decide you don't want page numbers, you must delete the page numbering code.

To delete page numbering

1. Move to the position where you invoked the page numbering function.

2. Press **Alt-F3**, or **F11** (**Reveal Codes**).

3. Delete the `[Pg Numbering:]` code.

You can turn off page numbering for the entire document or for a section of the document.

To turn off page numbering

1. Press **Shift-F8** (**Format**) to display the Format menu.

2. Press **2** or **P** to display the Format: Page menu.

3. Press **7** or **P** to select Page Numbering.

4. Press **9** or **N** for No Page Numbers.

5. Press **F7** (**Exit**) to return to your document.

You can suppress page numbering for a single page so that no number appears for that page but numbering continues on the following pages. For instance, you may not want the title page of a report to have a page number.

To suppress page numbering for a single page

1. Move to the top of the page on which you want numbering suppressed.

2. Press **Shift-F8** (**Format**) to display the Format menu.

3. Press **2** or **P** to display the Format: Page menu.

4. Press **9** or **U** to select Suppress (this page only).

5. Press **4** or **P** to Suppress Page Numbering.

6. Press **Y**.

7. Press **F7** (**Exit**) twice to return to your document.

Numbering Paragraphs

Paragraph Numbering differs from Outline because you must insert numbers manually. But, unlike Outline, Paragraph Numbering lets you choose the level number, regardless of the cursor position. Paragraph Numbering may be easier to edit if, for example, your document has few outline numbers and a great deal of text.

Just as you can define a numbering style for Outline, you can select a numbering style for Paragraph Numbering as well.

To Number Paragraphs

1. Move the cursor to the left margin of the paragraph you want to number.

2. Press **Shift-F5** (**Date/Outline**).

3. Press **5** or **P** to choose Para Num. WordPerfect prompts:

   ```
   Paragraph Level (Press Enter for
     Automatic):
   ```

4. Type the level number you want to assign and press **Enter**, or press **Enter**. If you press Enter for automatic numbering, the number or letter that WordPerfect inserts corresponds to the cursor position. With the cursor at the left margin, WordPerfect inserts a level 1 number; with the cursor at the first tab stop, WordPerfect inserts a level 2 number, and so on.

5. Complete Steps 1–4 for each of the paragraphs you want to number.

Outlines

WordPerfect's Outline feature permits you to create an outline and generate paragraph numbers automatically. Outlines in WordPerfect are simply normal text with a [Par Num] code inserted where each paragraph number appears in the printed document. Each time you press Enter, you create a new paragraph number. Within the line, each time you press Tab, you create a different level number.

The style you select determines the characters used for each level. The default paragraph numbering style is Outline (uppercase Roman numerals for level one, uppercase letters for level two, Arabic numbers for level three, and so on).

To create an outline

1. If you want to title your outline, press **Shift-F6** (**Center**), type the title, and press **Enter**.

2. Move the cursor to the position on the page where you want the outline to begin.

3. Press **Shift-F5** (**Date/Outline**). The following menu appears:

   ```
   1 Date Text; 2 Date Code; 3 Date
     Format; 4 Outline; 5 Para Num;
     6 Define: 0
   ```

4. Press **4** or **O** to turn on Outline.

5. Press **Enter** to insert the first paragraph number in the outline ("I." in Outline style).

6. To place the number and move the cursor, press **F4** (**Indent**); press the **space bar**; or press the **space bar** and **Tab**.

7. Type the text for the first entry.

8. Press **Enter** to move to the next line and automatically enter the next number. Press **Enter** again to insert a blank line if you want (the number moves down with the cursor).

9. Press **Tab** to move in one level. The number follows and changes to the next level number, "A." in Outline style.

10. To place the number and move the cursor, press **F4** (**Indent**), the **space bar**, or the **space bar** and then **Tab**.

11. Type the text for this entry and press **Enter**.

12. Follow Steps 5–11 to complete your outline.

If you press Tab too many times, you can move back a level by pressing Shift-Tab (Margin Release).

To turn off the outline feature

1. Press **Shift-F5** (**Date/Outline**).

2. Press **4** or **O** to choose Outline.

Outline levels are determined by tab stops and by the style of numbering selected. Outline is the default numbering style; you can change the numbering style.

To change the numbering style

1. Press **Shift-F5** (**Date/Outline**).

2. Press **6** or **D** to choose Define.

The Paragraph Number Definition menu appears.

3. Choose from the selection of predefined numbering styles (2 through 5 on the menu).

Or press **6** or **U** to select User-defined and to move the cursor to the Current Definition line. Then type each level number, press **Enter** to move to the next level, and press **F7** (**Exit**) when you complete your numbering definition.

4. Press **F7** (**Exit**) twice to return to your document.

Page Breaks

WordPerfect offers you several options for controlling where one page ends and the next begins. WordPerfect's automatic page breaks are based on 54 single-spaced lines of text on a 66-line page using the default margin settings. WordPerfect inserts a dashed line in your document on-screen wherever an automatic page break

occurs. These *soft page breaks* produce a hidden [SPg]
code. When you add or delete text from a page, soft
page breaks are recalculated automatically.

To force a page break at a certain spot, enter a *hard page
break*. The page always ends at that point. On-screen a
hard page break appears as a double-dashed line. In
Reveal Codes (Alt-F3, or F11), a hard page break
displays as [HPg].

You also can control where a page breaks with the
Conditional End of Page function, the Block Protect
command, and the Widows and Orphans feature.

To insert a hard page break

1. Move the cursor to the beginning of the text that
   should appear on a new page.

2. Press **Ctrl-Enter**.

To delete a hard page break

Move the cursor to the beginning of the line just below
the double-dashed line, and press **Backspace**.

Or move the cursor to the last space before the double-
dashed line, and press **Del**.

Or press **Alt-F3** or **F11** (**Reveal Codes**); delete the
[Hpg] code; and press **Alt-F3** or **F11** (**Reveal Codes**).

Be careful when you are using hard page breaks. If you
insert text into a page that ends with a hard page break,
the hard page break may move beyond the point at
which WordPerfect normally inserts a soft page break,
creating an extra page that has only a few lines.

To use the Conditional End of Page command

1. Count the lines that must remain together on the
   same page.

2. Move the cursor to the line above the lines you want to keep together.

3. Press **Shift-F8** (**Format**) to display the Format menu.

4. Select **4** or **O** to display the Format: Other menu.

5. Press **2** or **C** for Conditional End of Page. WordPerfect prompts:

   ```
   Number of Lines to Keep Together:
   ```

6. Type the number of lines you counted in Step 1 and press **Enter**.

7. Press **F7** (**Exit**) to return to your document.

The Conditional End of Page command groups a given number of lines so that they won't break across two pages. Use this command, for example, when you want to be sure that the title in a document is followed by at least three lines of text.

To use the block protect command

1. Press **Alt-F4**, or **F12** (**Block**).

2. Highlight the text you want to protect. When you define the block, move the cursor to the end of the block but don't include the final return at the end of a paragraph.

3. Press **Shift-F8** (**Format**). WordPerfect displays the following prompt:

   ```
   Protect block? (Y/N) No
   ```

4. Press **Y** to protect the block.

Notes

Block Protect is similar to Conditional End of Page, but

instead of specifying a number of lines, you define the
text you want to protect as a block. If you later add or
subtract lines from the block, WordPerfect keeps the
block on the same page.

WordPerfect can automatically prevent single lines from
being "stranded" at the top or at the bottom of a page.
The first line of a paragraph left at the bottom of a page
is called a *widow*; the last line of a paragraph left at the
top of a page is called an *orphan*. Activating the Widow/
Orphan Protection at the beginning of your document
prevents their occurrence throughout the entire
document.

To invoke Widow/Orphan Protection

1. Position the cursor at the top of the document (or
   wherever you want the protection to begin).

2. Press **Shift-F8 (Format)** to display the Format
   menu.

3. Press **1** or **L** to display the Format: Line menu.

4. Press **9** or **W** to select Widow/Orphan Protection.

5. Press **Y** to turn on Widow/Orphan Protection.

6. Press **F7 (Exit)** to return to your document.

Widow/Orphan Protection takes effect when you
activate it and remains in effect until you turn it off. To
turn off the feature, repeat Steps 1–4. Press **N** for Step 5.

Positioning Text

You control where text prints on the page by selecting
the paper size, setting top and bottom margins, and using
the Advance feature.

WordPerfect assumes that you use 8 1/2 by 11-inch paper and that your printer prints 6 lines per inch or 66 lines per page. (Legal-size 8 1/2 by 14-inch paper requires a setting of 84 lines per page.) If you use 8 1/2 by 11-inch paper, don't change anything. If you want to use legal-size paper, you can change the paper size. You can choose any of nine predefined paper sizes, or you can define your own size.

To change paper size and type

1. Press **Shift-F8** (**Format**) to display the Format menu.

2. Press **2** or **P** to display the Format: Page menu.

3. Press **8** or **S** to select Paper Size/Type. WordPerfect displays the Format: Paper Size menu.

4. Type the number associated with the paper size. For example, press **3** or **L** to select Legal.

After you choose a paper size, WordPerfect displays the Format: Paper Type menu. Some printers select forms from several physical locations. After you define your printer's form capabilities with the Forms feature on the Printer Settings menu, WordPerfect uses this information when it sees a Paper Size/Type code.

5. Choose a paper type from the predefined types listed.

6. Press **F7** (**Exit**) to return to your document.

If you select Other at the Paper Size menu, WordPerfect prompts for width and length measurements. Use this option to define your own paper size and type so that you can print on nonstandard-size paper.

WordPerfect is preset to leave 1-inch (6-line) margins at the top and bottom of the page, leaving 54 lines for text on 11-inch paper (72 lines on 14-inch legal paper). Page numbers, headers, footers, and footnotes must fit within the allotted 54- or 72-line text area. In a 2-line footer, the second line is placed on line 61 (11-inch paper) or line 79 (14-inch paper).

To change the top and bottom margins

1. Move the cursor to the position in your document where you want to set margins—usually at the beginning of the document.

2. Press **Shift-F8** (**Format**) to display the Format menu.

3. Press **2** or **P** to display the Format: Page menu.

4. Press **5** or **M** to select Margins (Top/Bottom).

5. Type a new top margin in decimal inches and press **Enter**. If, for example, you want a top margin of 1 1/2 inches, type 1.5 and press **Enter**.

6. Type a new bottom margin in decimal inches and press **Enter**.

7. Press **F7** (**Exit**) to return to your document.

You can use WordPerfect's Advance feature to insert in your document a code that instructs your printer to move left, right, up, or down before printing. You also can use Advance to tell your printer to start printing at a specific location on the page. (Some printers can't "advance" backwards.) Advance provides a way to move text down on the page to compensate for letterheads and logos on starting pages.

To use Advance

1. Position the cursor at the location where you want Advance to begin.

2. Press **Shift-F8** (**Format**) to display the Format menu.

3. Press **4** or **O** to display the Format: Other menu.

4. Press **1** or **A** to choose Advance. You can advance up, down, right, left, or to a specified position.

5. Type the number associated with your selection.

6. Type the distance (in decimal inches) to advance and press **Enter**. The distance you enter for Advance Up or Advance Down is relative to the current cursor position. If you choose Position, the number you enter specifies an absolute position on the page.

7. Press **F7** (**Exit**) to return to your document.

To return the print head to its original position, enter a separate code to advance in the opposite direction.

Previewing a Document

Use the View Document feature to view your document before printing it. You'll save costly printer paper and time by first previewing your document, making changes if needed, and then printing the document when you're certain it's perfect. Document pages appear on-screen as they'll appear when printed on paper including graphics (if your system can display graphics), footnotes, page numbers, line numbers, headers, footers, and justification.

To Preview Your Document

1. Position the cursor anywhere on the page you want to view.

2. Press **Shift-F7** (**Print**).

3. Press **6** or **V** to view the document.

4. Press **1** (100%) to view the document at its actual
    size; or press **2** (200%) to view the document at
    twice its actual size; or press **3** (Full Page) to view
    the entire page; or press **4** (Facing Pages) to view
    the current page and its facing page (odd-numbered
    pages are displayed on the right side of the screen,
    even-numbered pages on the left).

5. Press PgUp or PgDn to view other pages of the
    document.

6. Press **F7** (**Exit**) to return to your document.

Print Cartridges & Fonts

Many printers let you choose a typeface (*font*) by
selecting a plug-in print cartridge or daisywheel or by
downloading a font file from your disk. The Cartridges
and Fonts feature on the Printer Settings menu lists the
fonts that WordPerfect can use with your printer. You
can mark the fonts you plan to use; these fonts will
appear on the Base Font and Initial Font menus.

To install cartridges and fonts

1. Press **Shift-F7** (**Print**).

2. Press **S** to choose Select Printer.

3. Use the cursor keys to highlight the name of the
    printer you want to edit.

4. Press **3** or **E** to choose Edit.

5. Insert the Printer disk with the definition file for the
    current printer in drive A.

6. Press 5 or C to choose Cartridges and Fonts. WordPerfect displays the Select Printer: Cartridges and Fonts menu. If you can't remember which disk contains your printer definition, insert each Printer disk and press 5 or C until the menu appears.

7. Move the cursor to a font category.

8. Press 1 or F to choose Select Fonts. WordPerfect displays another Select Printer: Cartridges and Fonts menu.

9. Move the cursor to a cartridge or font that you want to use with your printer. Press * (asterisk) to mark the font as `Present when print job begins`, or press + (plus) to mark the font as Can be loaded during print job.

Mark the font `Present when print job begins` if the font or cartridge will always be loaded and available when you start a print job. Fonts marked with an asterisk will be downloaded when you choose the Initialize Printer option on the Print menu.

Mark the font `Can be loaded during print job` if you want WordPerfect to load the font (or prompt you to insert a cartridge or daisywheel) when it encounters the font code in a document. WordPerfect will reset the printer to the Initial Font at the end of the print job.

10. Press F7 (Exit) five times to return to the editing screen.

Fonts marked with both an asterisk (*) and plus sign (+) are automatically downloaded at the start of a print job and, if necessary, unloaded in order to load another font. If you unload the font, it will be loaded again at the end of the job. To download soft fonts marked "initially present," press Shift-F7 (Print) and press 7 or I to choose Initialize Printer.

Printer Selection

After starting WordPerfect, the first thing you should do
is select your printer. *Selecting your printer* simply
means telling WordPerfect what make and model printer
you'll be using to print your documents.

Reminders

WordPerfect and the printer *must* be linked properly. If
they are not, they cannot communicate; and if they do
not communicate, the printer will not print your
documents.

A *printer definition* is not the same thing as a *printer*.
Printer definitions are software; printers are hardware. A
printer definition tells WordPerfect how to control a
certain make and model of printer. You may install and
have available for selection (from the Select Printer
menu) only six printer definitions at one time.

To Select Your Printer

1. If you are using a hard disk, insert the 5 1/4-inch
    master disk Printer 1 or the 3 1/2-inch Printer 1/
    Printer 2 master disk into drive A.

    If you are using a dual floppy disk system, insert into
    drive B the 5 1/4-inch Printer 1–Working disk or the
    3 1/2-inch Printer 1/Printer 2–Working disk.

2. Start WordPerfect.

3. Press **Shift-F7** (**Print**).

4. Press **S** to choose Select Printer(s). The Print: Select
    Printer screen is displayed.

5. Press **1** or **A** to choose Additional Printers. The
    Select Printer: Additional Printers screen is
    displayed with a message that says `Printer
    files not found.`

6. Press **2** or **O** to choose Other Disk. WordPerfect prompts: `Directory for printer files:` followed by the current drive and directory name.

7. Type **a:** if you are using a hard disk, or type **b:** if you are using a dual floppy system. A list of the available printer devices on this printer disk is displayed.

If the name of your printer does not appear on the list of additional printers, insert another Printer disk and press **2** or **O** to view a second list of printers until you find the printer you want.

8. Move the cursor to the name of the printer you want to add and press **Enter**, or press **1** or **S** and press **Enter**.

WordPerfect can assign printer definitions to as many as six different printers. Right now you are assigning a printer model definition to what WordPerfect thinks is the first of six printers.

9. Press **Enter** to accept the displayed name, or type a name of your own and press **Enter**.

10. Read the information on the Printer Helps and Hints Screen.

11. Press **F7** (**Exit**) to move to the Select Printer: Edit menu.

12. Enter the information required, such as assigning a proper printer port or initial font.

13. Press **F7** (**Exit**) twice to return to the Print menu.

The port is the socket on the back of your computer to which your printer is connected. Most printers are parallel printers and are connected to the LPT1 port. (The first parallel port is LPT1; the second, if you have one, is LPT2.) Serial printers are connected to ports COM1 and COM2. You might want to change your printer's port setting if, for example, you have more than one printer attached to your system.

Printing

Printing from the Screen

With WordPerfect, you can print all or part of the document that currently appears on-screen directly from the screen, or you can print all or part of a document you have previously stored to disk. From the screen, you can print the entire document, a single page, or a marked block of text.

To print the entire document from the screen

1. Place the cursor anywhere in the document.

2. Press **Shift-F7** (**Print**) to display the Print menu.

3. Press **1** or **F** to choose the Full Document option.

To print a single page from the displayed document

1. Place the cursor anywhere in the page you want to print.

2. Press **Shift-F7** (**Print**).

3. Press **2** or **P** to select Page.

If the page you've selected doesn't appear near the

beginning of the document, you may notice a short
pause before the page prints. WordPerfect scans the
pages for the last format settings for margins, tabs, and
so on.

To print a block of text from the screen

1. Move the cursor to the first character of the block
   of text you plan to print.

2. Press **Alt-F4,** or **F12 (Block).** The message `Block`
   `on` flashes in the lower left corner of your screen.

3. Move the cursor to the character space immediately
   following the last character of the block of text you
   plan to print.

4. Press **Shift-F7 (Print).** The prompt `Print`
   `block?` `(Y/N)` appears at the bottom of your
   screen.

5. Press **Y** to print.

Printing from a Disk

With WordPerfect, you can print a document from disk
without displaying it on-screen. You can print from
either the Print menu or the List Files menu.

Reminders

If the file you're printing is stored on a floppy disk,
don't remove it from the disk drive until the print job
has finished.

If you are using the Fast Save feature, you cannot print a
document from the disk; you must first retrieve the
document to the screen.

To use the Print menu to print a document from disk

1. Press **Shift-F7** (**Print**).

2. Press **3** or **D** to select Document on Disk. The
   prompt Document name: appears.

3. Type the file name and press **Enter**. Or, if the
   document is stored in a different directory than the
   current directory, type the drive, path and file name,
   and press **Enter**. Pages: (All) displays on the
   status line.

4. Press **Enter** to print the entire document, or type
   the pages you want to print and press **Enter**.

WordPerfect reads the file from disk, creates a print job,
and adds the document to the print queue.

In addition to printing from the Print menu, you can
print from the List Files screen. Printing from the List
Files screen has two advantages: you don't need to
remember the name of the file you want to print, and
you can mark any number of files to print. The files are
printed in the order in which you mark them.

To use the List Files screen to print a document from disk

1. Press **F5** (**List Files**).

2. If the file resides in the current drive and directory,
   press **Enter**; or if the file is in a differnt directory,
   type the drive, path and file name and press **Enter**.

3. Use the cursor keys to highlight the name of the file
   you want to print.

Or press **N** and begin typing the name of the file. When
the file you want is highlighted, press **Enter**.

4. Press **4** or **P** to select Print. Pages: (All)
   displays on the status line.

5. Press **Enter** to print the entire document, or type
   the pages you want to print and press **Enter**.

To mark several files to print from the List Files screen
1. Press **F5** (**List Files**).

2. Use the cursor keys to highlight the name of the file
   you want to print.

3. Press * (asterisk) to mark each file you want to
   print.

4. After you've marked each file, type **4** or **P** to select
   Print. WordPerfect prompts:

   ```
   Print marked files? (Y/N) No
   ```

5. Press **Y**.

WordPerfect adds the files to the printing queue and
prints them in the order in which you selected the files.

Using the Control Printer Menu

WordPerfect's Control Printer feature is a powerful tool
for managing your printing activities. You can, with
Control Printer, cancel individual print jobs or all print
jobs, display a list of jobs waiting to be printed, move a
print job to the top of the list, and temporarily suspend
and then resume printing if your printer has jammed or
needs a new ribbon.

To cancel a print job while it's printing
1. Press **Shift-F7** (**Print**).

2. Press **4** or **C** to choose Control Printer and display
   the Control Printer menu.

3. Press **1** or **C** to choose Cancel Job(s). WordPerfect
   displays the following message (the number of the
   job currently printing is included in the prompt):

   ```
   Cancel which job? (*=All Jobs)
   ```

4. Press **Enter** to cancel the current job in the queue;
   or type the number of the job you want to cancel; or
   press * (asterisk) to cancel all the jobs in the queue
   and press **Y** to confirm the cancellation.

You can use the Rush Print Job option to interrupt the
current print job so that you can print another job in the
queue or to print the rush job after the current job is
printed. If you elect to interrupt the job currently
printing, the document will automatically resume
printing after the rush job is done.

To rush a print job

1. Press **Shift-F7** (**Print**).

2. Press **4** or **C** to select Control Printer.

3. Press **2** or **R** to select Rush Job. WordPerfect
   displays the following message:

   ```
   Rush which job?
   ```

4. Type the number of the print job you want to
   move up.

5. Press **Y** if you want to interrupt the current printing
   job, or press **N** or **Enter** to print the job after the
   current job is finished printing.

To stop printing temporarily

1. Press **Shift-F7** (**Print**).

2. Press **4** or **C** to select Control Printer.

3. Press **5** or **S** to choose Stop.

4. Make the desired corrections; then position the print head at the top of the next page.

5. Press **4** or **G** to choose Go (start printer). Printing resumes on page one if your document consists of only one page or if you stopped printing on page one. Otherwise, WordPerfect will prompt you to enter the page number where you want printing to resume.

6. Type the page number (if prompted) and press **Enter**.

If you're printing on hand-fed single sheets or if you specified manual when you selected the printer, the printer does not start printing immediately after you've given the Print command. Instead, the printer pauses before printing each page to give you time to insert a sheet of paper. To start the first sheet, you must go back to the Control Printer screen.

To print on hand-fed paper

1. Press **Shift-F7** (**Print**).

2. Press **1** or **F** to select Full Document.

3. Press **Shift-F7** (**Print**) again.

4. Press **4** or **C** to choose Control Printer.

5. Press **4** or **G** to select Go once you have the paper aligned.

Using Your Printer as a Typewriter

With WordPerfect you can use your printer as a typewriter. This feature is useful when you need to write a brief note or address an envelope. WordPerfect can send each character to the printer immediately after you type it or wait until you press Enter to send the line.

To Use Type Through

1. Press Shift-F7 (Print).

2. Press 5 or Y to select Type Through. The following message appears at the bottom of your screen:

   ```
   Type Through by: 1 Line; 2
     Character
   ```

3. Press 1 or L for Line to send the line to the printer when you press Enter. You can edit the line if you select this option.

Or press 2 or C for Character to send characters to the printer as you type. If you make a typing mistake, you cannot correct it.

4. Type the text. If you select Line, you can use the cursor keys and the Backspace and Delete keys to edit the line of text. The top line of the screen shows the previous line of text, which you cannot edit. To copy the top line to the bottom (current editing) line, press Ctrl-F4.

5. If you chose Line, press Enter to send the line to the printer.

Or, if you chose Character, WordPerfect sends each character to the printer as you press the key. To clear the current line of text from your screen, press Ctrl-PgDn.

6. Press F7 (Exit) twice to return to the editing screen.

Printing with Sheet Feeders

A sheet feeder supplies paper to the printer from one or more bins. Before you can use a sheet feeder, you must select a sheet feeder definition for your printer.

To Select a Sheet Feeder

1. Press **Shift-F7** (**Print**).

2. Press **S** to choose Select Printer.

3. Use the cursor keys to highlight the name of the printer you want to edit.

4. Press **3** or **E** to choose Edit.

5. Press **3** or **S** to choose Sheet Feeder. WordPerfect displays the following prompt:

   ```
   Directory for printer files:
   ```

6. Insert the printer disk that contains the definition for your printer in drive A.

7. Type **a:** and press **Enter**. The Select Printer: Sheet Feeder menu appears. If you can't remember which disk contains your printer definition, insert each of the printer disks and type **a:** until the menu appers.

8. Move the cursor to the name of the desired sheet feeder and press **Enter**, **1**, or **S** to choose Select. Or press **2** or **O** to choose None and exit the menu.

After you select a definition, WordPerfect displays a Sheet Feeder Helps and Hints screen for the sheet feeder you've selected.

9. Press **F7** (**Exit**) four times to return to your document.

Selecting Number of Copies, Binding Width, and Print Quality

You select binding width, number of copies, and graphics and text quality from the Print menu.

WordPerfect will print the number of copies you selected for all print jobs until you change the Number of Copies back to 1.

Binding Width is the extra space added at the inside edge of each page when the document is printed. Setting a binding width shifts odd-numbered pages to the right and even-numbered pages to the left by the specified amount. The binding option provides an extra margin along the inside edge of the paper to allow for binding or three-hole drilling the final copy.

The Graphics Quality option controls the degree of resolution (sharpness) your printer uses to print graphics images.

Changing the Initial Font

The initial font is the typeface style and sizes that WordPerfect uses to print standard text and around which other fonts are defined. Enhancements (boldface, italics, small caps, and so on) are variations of the current font. For example, if the current font is Times Roman and you use the Italics option on the Appearance menu, the text will be printed in Times Roman Italics.

To change the Initial Font

1. Press **Shift-F7** (**Print**).

2. Press **S** to choose Select Printer.

3. Use the cursor keys to highlight the name of the printer you want to edit.

4. Press **3** or **E** to choose Edit.

5. Press **6** or **I** to choose Initial Font. WordPerfect displays the Select Printer: Initial Font menu.

6. Use the cursor keys to highlight the name of a font and press **Enter**, **1**, or **S** to select the font.

7. Press **F7** (**Exit**) three times to return to the editing screen.

Redline and Strikeout

Redlining is a method of marking text that's been edited, added to, or deleted from a document. When several people work on a document, redlining is a useful way to let everyone know what changes are proposed.

In WordPerfect you can choose how redlining appears on the printed page. With many printers, redline appears as a mark in the margin next to the redlined text. With other printers redlined text appears shaded or highlighted. If you have a color printer, redlined text prints red.

While redlining is generally used to identify text that needs to be expanded or illustrated, WordPerfect's *strikeout* feature is used to identify text that the editor believes should be deleted. Strikeout appears as characters superimposed over other characters.

To select the redlining method

1. Press **Shift-F8** (**Format**) to display the Format menu.

2. Press **3** or **D** to display the Format: Document menu.

3. Press **4** or **R** to select Redline Method.

4. Press **1** or **P** to select Printer Dependent which
    marks redline text according to your printer's
    definition of redlining.

Or press **2** or **L** to select Left which prints a character in
the margin to the left of the redlined text.

Or press **3** or **A** to select Alternating which prints a
redline character in the outside margins of alternating
pages.

5. Press **F7** (**Exit**) to return to your document.

To redline or strikeout text

1. Press **Alt-F4**, or **F12** (**Block**).

2. Highlight the block you want to redline.

3. Press **Ctrl-F8** (**Font**). The Font menu appears at the
    bottom of your screen.

4. Press **2** or **A** to select Appearance.

5. Press **8** or **R** to select Redline, or press **9** or **S** to
    select Strikeout.

Remember that when you remove strikeout text, you are
deleting the actual text marked for strikeout, not just the
strikeout symbol.

References

To guide your readers to related information in the
document, WordPerfect's Automatic Reference feature
allows you to reference page numbers, footnote
numbers, section numbers, endnote numbers, and
graphics box numbers. If you make changes, the
references are renumbered automatically.

You create an automatic reference using two types of codes: a *reference code* marks the place you make the reference, and a *target code* marks the place to which you refer. For example, on page 10, if you refer to related information on page 20, place the reference code on page 10 and the target code on page 20.

To mark both the reference and the target

1. Move the cursor to the position where you want to create an automatic reference.

2. Type the introductory text and press the **space bar**.

3. Press **Alt-F5** (**Mark Text**) to display the following menu:

   ```
   1 Auto Ref; 2 Subdoc; 3 Index;
   4 ToA Short Form; 5 Define;
   6 Generate: 0
   ```

4. Press **1** or **R** to choose Auto Ref and display the Mark Text: Automatic Reference menu.

5. Press **3** or **B** to choose Mark Both Reference and Text. The Tie Reference to: menu appears.

6. Type the number that represents the type of target for the reference you are creating. (If you select Graphics Box Number, select the type of box you are referencing from the menu.)

7. Move your cursor to the target and press **Enter**. WordPerfect prompts:

   ```
   Target Name:
   ```

8. Type a name for the target and press **Enter**.

WordPerfect marks the reference, as well as the target, with the name you select for the target. When you press Enter, WordPerfect returns the cursor to the position of the Reference code and inserts the target page number. Instead of marking the reference and the target at the same time, you can mark each separately.

To mark the reference only

1. Follow Steps 1–4 for marking both reference and target.

2. Press **1** or **R** to choose Mark Reference.

3. Type the number of the type of target.

4. Type a name for the target and press **Enter**.

In the reference code, WordPerfect enters a question mark. When you name a target with the same name you've chosen for this reference and generate the references, WordPerfect automatically replaces the question mark with the number of the target.

To mark the target only

1. Follow Steps 1–4 for marking both reference and target.

2. Press **2** or **T** to choose Mark Target.

3. Type a name for the target and press **Enter**.

WordPerfect generates reference numbers when you enter a reference and target at the same time. But, if you mark targets and references separately, or if you make editing changes, you need to generate references to update the reference numbers.

To generate automatic references, press **Alt-F5** (**Mark Text**) and select **6** or **G** to choose Generate.

Repeating Values

Some of the keys on your keyboard automatically repeat when you hold down the key. Many other WordPerfect functions can be repeated only with the aid of the Esc key.

To Repeat a Character or a Cursor-Movement Key

1. Move the cursor to the location where you want the character or cursor-movement key repeated.

2. Press Esc (Escape). The prompt Repeat Value=8 appears in the lower left corner of the screen. The preset repeat value is 8, but it can be changed for one occurrence or for the entire work session.

3. Type the repeat value if 8 is not the correct number of repetitions.

4. Press the character or cursor-movement key to be repeated.

Retrieving Files

You can retrieve documents stored on disk in two ways: press Shift-F10 (Retrieve) or press F5 (List Files) to use the List Files screen. The List Files screen displays a two-column alphabetized list of your files, including the file size and the date and time each file was last saved.

Reminders

If you do not clear your screen before retrieving a document, WordPerfect attaches the retrieved file to the document displayed on-screen. Use F7 (Exit) to clear the old document before retrieving the new document.

Never try to retrieve WordPerfect system (program) files. Trying to view them while WordPerfect is running can cause serious damage to the files.

If you decide that you do not want to retrieve a file,
press F1 (Cancel).

To use the Retrieve command

1. Press **Shift-F10** (**Retrieve**). The following prompt
   is displayed:

   ```
   Document to be retrieved:
   ```

2. Type the name of the document and press **Enter**. If
   the document is password-protected, WordPerfect
   prompts:

   ```
   Enter Password (FILENAME):
   ```

3. Type the password you assigned to the file, and
   then press **Enter**.

If the message ERROR: File Not Found displays,
either you have typed the name incorrectly or the file
doesn't exist in the directory. Type the name again. If
you cannot remember the name of the document you
want to retrieve, use the List Files screen.

To use the List Files screen

1. Press **F5** (**List Files**). WordPerfect displays a file
   specification similar to the following in the lower
   left corner of the screen:

   ```
   Dir C:\WP50\*.*
   ```

2. To view the documents stored on the named drive,
   press **Enter**.

Or, to view files on a drive other than the one
designated, type the letter of the disk drive, a colon, and
the path name. Then press **Enter**.

The List Files menu appears. WordPerfect provides two
ways to specify file names.

3. Use the arrow keys to move the highlight bar to the file you want to retrieve.

Or press **N** for Name Search and type the file name. As you type the file name, the cursor moves the highlight bar to the name of the file you want to retrieve. Press **Enter** or an arrow key to end the name search.

4. Press **1** or **R** to select the Retrieve option from the menu displayed at the bottom of your screen.

Reveal Codes

Many times when you press a key in WordPerfect, a *hidden code* is inserted into the text. The term hidden is used because you cannot see that code on-screen. Such codes tell WordPerfect when to execute tabs, margin settings, hard returns, indents, and so on. Some hidden codes turn on and off features, such as Math or Columns. And, some codes work as a pair, such as the codes for bold, underline, and italic. The first code in a pair acts as a toggle switch to turn on a feature; the second code serves to turn off the feature. These hidden codes are called Reveal Codes.

To see the Reveal Codes

1. Press **Alt-F3**, or **F11** (**Reveal Codes**). The screen splits in half. The same text is displayed in both windows except the text at the bottom half includes the hidden codes. The bar between screens displays the tab and margin settings for the line on which the cursor rests.

2. Press **Alt-F3**, or **F11** (**Reveal Codes**) again to restore the normal screen.

Editing in Reveal Codes is a little different from editing in the document editing screen. The cursor in the upper window looks the same; the cursor in the lower window displays as a highlighted bar. When the cursor comes upon a hidden code (in the lower window), the cursor expands to cover the entire code. In the upper window, you see only a blank space.

Hidden codes can be deleted in the normal typing screen or in the Reveal Codes screen. Because you can see the codes in the Reveal Codes screen, deleting them with Reveal Codes is easier.

As you delete codes from the Reveal Codes screen, notice that the effect of your changes is reflected in the upper portion of the screen. In Reveal Codes mode, you can enter commands and text and immediately observe the position of any new hidden codes.

To delete Reveal Codes

1. Move the cursor to the place in your document where the code is likely to be located.

2. Press **Alt-F3**, or **F11** (**Reveal Codes**).

3. Use the arrow keys to position the cursor on the hidden code.

4. Press **Del** to delete the hidden code.

5. To return to the normal typing screen, press **Alt-F3**, or **F11** (**Reveal Codes**) again.

Saving Documents

What you see on-screen is a *temporary* display; only the documents you have transferred to disk storage enjoy a measure of security. Should something interrupt the power to your computer (a storm, a power cord pulled from the wall, a power surge), any text you haven't saved to disk is gone forever!

As a rule, you should *save your work every 10 or 15 minutes*. Remember that you can press F10 (Save) at any time while you are working on your document.

File names have two parts. The first part of the name can contain from one to eight characters (numbers, letters, and some punctuation marks). The second part (called the *extension*) can contain no more than three characters. The first part of the file name is separated from its extension by a period (.). For example, in the file name LETTER1.JIM, the extension is .JIM. Use the extension to categorize files.

If you are using a hard disk system, the program, system, and document files usually reside on drive C. When you press F10 (Save), the prompt includes the disk drive and directory designation.

Most hard disk drive users make subdirectories to organize and store different kinds of documents. For example, you may have a subdirectory called WPLETTER in which you save correspondence or a subdirectory called WPMEMO in which you save interoffice memos. WordPerfect permits you to create directories with the List Files feature.

On a dual floppy disk system, drive A is reserved for program and system data. Do not save documents on drive A. Instead start the program from drive A and make drive B your default drive for your documents.

To save and name your documents

1. Press **F10 (Save)**. The following prompt appears:

   ```
   Document to be saved:
   ```

   If you have saved the document previously, the file name follows the prompt.

2. Press **Enter** to keep the name that appears in the prompt. Or, to save the file in the current directory,

type a file name and press **Enter**. To save the file in
another subdirectory, type the path name and the
file name and press **Enter**.

You may type the name in either uppercase or lowercase
letters; WordPerfect converts what you type to
uppercase.

If you just press Enter or type the name of an existing
file, this prompt appears on-screen:

```
Replace C:\WP\LETTER.JLS (Y/N) No
```

3. If you want to replace the old file with the file on-
    screen, press **Y**.

Or, if you don't want to replace the old file on the disk
(for instance, you want to save both the new and the old
versions of your letter), press **N** or press **Enter**. Then
give the new version a different name.

The Screen Display

WordPerfect displays your document almost exactly as it
will appear when it is printed. What you see on-screen is
approximately one-half of a standard typed page. The
main portion of the screen displays the document.

The line of information that appears at the bottom of the
screen is called the *status line*, because that information
describes the cursor's status. The left side of the status
line shows the current document's name. From time to
time, the document name is replaced temporarily by
system messages and prompts.

The second item in the status line (Doc) indicates which
of two available documents is currently displayed on-
screen. WordPerfect is able to hold two documents in
memory simultaneously. The documents are identified
as either Doc 1 or Doc 2.

Pg identifies the number of the page on which the cursor currently rests.

Ln indicates the number of the line, in inches, centimeters, points, or lines (on your document page), on which the cursor rests. You can change the units used for the status line display by selecting that option on the Setup menu (press Shift-F1 to display the Setup menu).

Pos tells you in which column on your document's page the cursor lies. The Pos indicator serves the following functions as well: (1) the Pos indicator appears in uppercase letters (POS) if the Caps Lock key is activated for typing in uppercase letters; (2) when the Pos indicator blinks, the Num Lock key is activated so that you can use the numeric keypad to type numbers; (3) when you create or move through boldface letters, the position indicator number changes from regular type to boldface type; (4) when the cursor moves into underlined or double-underlined text, the position indicator number reflects the enhancement of the text.

Status line information appears only on-screen; it does not appear in your printed document.

Search and Replace

WordPerfect makes two powerful tools available to you every time you begin your editing tasks—Search and Replace.

Using Search

The Search feature enables you to search for a single character, word, phrase, or sentence in either a forward or reverse direction from the location of your cursor. The group of characters or words you want to locate is called a *string*.

WordPerfect differentiates between upper- and lowercase characters only if you type uppercase characters in the search string. If you type the string in lowercase, WordPerfect looks for *either* upper- or lowercase characters. For example, if you ask the program to find *search*, WordPerfect stops at *search*, *Search*, and *SEARCH*. But if you ask the program to find *Search*, it stops only at the word *Search*.

Reminders

Be careful how you enter a search string. For example, if you enter the string the, WordPerfect matches your string to every occurrence of the word the as well as words that contain the string, such as anesthesia. To locate only the word the, enter a space before and after the word: <space>the<space>.

If you think that the string you're looking for might be in a header, footer, footnote, endnote, graphic box caption, or text box, you must perform an *extended search*. An extended search is the same as a regular search except that you must press Home, F2 for an extended forward search, and Home, Shift-F2 for an extended backward search.

If you need to find a hidden code, such as a margin setting, use the normal search procedure, but when the Srch: prompt appears, press the function key that creates the hidden code. When the search finds the hidden code, press Alt-F3 (Reveal Codes) to view the code and perform any editing.

When searching for paired codes, you can insert an ending code at the search (or replace) prompt by pressing the corresponding function key twice—for example, press F6 (Bold) once to insert a [BOLD] code, twice to insert [bold]. To remove the [BOLD] code, delete it with the cursor and Del keys.

If you are searching for text which includes an element that changes from one occurrence to the next—for example, (1), (2), (3)—or if you are uncertain about the correct spelling of a word, use the matching character ^X (press Ctrl-V, Ctrl- X). This *wild card* character matches any single character within a character string. Enter (^X) at the Æ Srch: prompt, and the cursor will stop at (1), (2), (3), (4), and so on. When you are uncertain about the spelling, enter **c^Xt** at the Æ Srch: prompt, and the cursor will stop at *cat, CAT, Cat, cot, cattle, cutting,* and so on. Be as specific about your character string as you can.

To find a word at the end of a paragraph, type the word at the Srch: prompt, along with any following punctuation, and then press Enter to insert a [HRt] code. For example, type **Einstein.[HRt].** The search finds only occurrences of **Einstein** that are followed by a period and a hard return (Enter key).

To Use Search

1. Press **F2 (Forward Search)** to search from the cursor position forward to the end of the document, or press **Shift-F2 (Backward Search)** to search from the end of the document to the beginning.

If you have selected Forward Search, the following prompt appears at the lower left corner of the screen:

→ Srch:

If you have selected Backward Search, the following prompt appears:

→ Srch:

2. Type the text string or code you want to find. You may type as many as 60 characters in your text string.

3. Press **F2** or **Esc** to begin the search. At this point
   F2 works for both Forward and Backward Search.

When WordPerfect finds the first occurrence of the
search target, the search stops. You can edit and move
around in the document freely.

If you want to continue the search, repeat Steps 1 and 3.
You don't need to retype your search string or code
because WordPerfect remembers your last search
request.

If WordPerfect can't find the search text, a * Not
Found * message is displayed.

To return the cursor to its location before the search,
press **Ctrl-Home** (**GoTo**) twice.

Caution

A common mistake is to press Enter instead of F2
(Forward Search) or Esc to exit the Srch: prompt.
Pressing Enter inserts a [HRt] code in the search string,
which may not be what you intended.

Using Replace

WordPerfect's Replace feature automatically finds every
occurrence of a string or code and replaces it with
another string or code. You also can use Replace to
remove a string or code completely.

To replace a string

1. Press **Alt-F2** (**Replace**). The following prompt
   appears in the lower left corner of the screen:

   w/Confirm? (Y/N) No

2. Press **Y** if you want to approve each replacement
   separately, or press **N** or **Enter** if you want all
   occurrences replaced without confirming them.

3. At the → `Srch:` prompt, type your search string.

4. Press **F2** (**Forward Search**) or **Esc**. The following prompt appears:

   `Replace with:`

5. If you want the string replaced, type the replacement string; or, if you want the search string deleted and not replaced with anything, go directly to Step 6.

6. Press **F2** (**Forward Search**) or **Esc**.

If you pressed **Y** at the `w/Confirm?` `(Y/N)` `No` prompt, the cursor stops at each occurrence of the search string and WordPerfect prompts: `Confirm?` `(Y/N)` `No`. Press **Y** to replace, and **N** to not replace. If you want to cancel the search and replace operation, press **F1** (**Cancel**). Otherwise, when all the occurrences have been replaced, the cursor stops.

7. To return to the position of the cursor before the Replace operation began, press **Ctrl-Home** twice.

To replace hidden codes

1. Press **Alt-F2** (**Replace**).

2. Press **Y** if you want to confirm each replacement, or press **N** if you want all occurrences replaced automatically.

3. When the Srch: prompt appears, press the desired function key—for example, press **F6** (**Bold**).

4. At the **Replace with:** prompt, type the replacement string; or, to delete the hidden code and not replace it with anything, go directly to Step 5.

5. Press **F2** (**Forward Search**) to begin the Replace operation.

Sort & Select

WordPerfect's Sort and Select feature has enough power and versatility to handle most recordkeeping tasks. Examples of two simple applications of the Sort command are sorting lines to create alphabetical phone lists or rosters, and sorting mailing lists by ZIP code to conform with postal service rules for large mailings.

WordPerfect can maneuver three kinds of records: a line, a paragraph, or a secondary merge record file. A line record ends with a hard or soft return, and a paragraph record ends with two hard returns. A secondary merge file contains records, each of which has fields. A field ends with a ^R merge code, and a record ends with a ^E merge code.

Before you can tell WordPerfect how you want to sort or select information, you need to understand the terms used by these functions.

Sorting Files

You can sort files displayed on-screen or files stored on disk, and you can return the sorted results to the screen or to a new file on disk. Sort works with three kinds of data: line, paragraph, and a secondary merge file. You must use a different type of sort for each kind of database. Use line sort when records are lines (a name or an item, for example); use paragraph sort when records are paragraphs (as in a standard legal clause, perhaps); and use merge sort when records are a secondary merge file (a list of names and addresses, for instance).

To Perform a Sort

1. If you want to sort a file while it's displayed on-screen, retrieve the desired file to your screen.

2. Press **Ctrl-F9 (Merge/Sort)**. WordPerfect displays
   the Merge/Sort menu:

   ```
   1 Merge; 2 Sort; 3 Sort Order: 0
   ```

3. Press **2** or **S** to choose Sort. The following prompt
   appears in the lower left corner of the screen:

   ```
   Input file to sort: (Screen)
   ```

4. Press **Enter** if you want to sort the file already
   displayed on-screen, or type the input file name if
   you want to sort a file stored on disk. The following
   prompt appears in the lower left corner of the
   screen:

   ```
   Output file for sort: (Screen)
   ```

5. Press **Enter** if you want the sorted results to replace
   the screen display, or type the output file name if
   you want the sorted results saved to disk in a new
   file.

Tabs must be set for fields. Set one tab per field with no
unused tabs between fields. Notice the tab ruler just
above the legend Sort by Line. If the tabs in the tab bar
do not reflect your one-tab-per-field setting, press **2** or **V**
to select View. The cursor moves into your document,
which is displayed in the top half of the split screen.
Move the cursor to the middle of a line of data. The tab
ruler should change to reflect your tab settings. Press **F7**
(**Exit**) to return to the Sort screen.

6. Press **7** or **T** to choose Type. WordPerfect displays
   the Type menu:

   ```
   Type: 1 Merge; 2 Line; 3
   Paragraph: 0
   ```

7. Select the type of records you are sorting: a
   secondary merge file (**1**), document lines (**2**), or
   paragraphs (**3**).

8. Press **6** or **O** to choose Order. WordPerfect displays
    the Direction menu:

    ```
    Direction: 1 Ascending; 2
    Descending: 0
    ```

9. Press **1** or **A** to choose Ascending for A-to-Z sort
    order, or press **2** or **D** to choose Descending for
    Z-to-A sort order.

10. Press **3** or **K** to choose Keys. WordPerfect displays
    the Keys menu:

    ```
    Type: a = Alphanumeric; n =
    Numeric;
    Use arrows; Press Exit when done
    ```

The cursor moves under the a in the Typ column so that
you can enter the location of each sort key.

11. Type **a** to specify an alphanumeric sort for Key1, or
    type **n** to specify a numeric sort for Key1.

12. Enter the location of Key1.

13. If you want to sort on more than one field, press the
    → key to move to the entry area for Key2.

You might choose more than one sort key if, for
example, you wanted to sort a mailing list in ZIP code
order, but you also wanted the last names sorted within
each ZIP code. You would therefore make the ZIP code
field Key1, and the last names Key2. Notice that the Typ
is *a* (alphanumeric) for all the keys, including ZIP codes,
because ZIP codes that begin with a zero (such as
00432) won't sort properly if you choose the numeric
type (Typ = n).

14. Enter the key location for Key2.

15. Move to and enter information for other keys.

16. Press F7 (Exit) to return to the Sort and Select menu.

17. To start the sort, press 1 or P to choose Perform Action.

Sorting Lines and Paragraphs

WordPerfect can sort the lines and paragraphs in any standard text file. This feature is particularly useful when you want to sort through office phone lists, personnel rosters, columns on charts, dated paragraphs, and so on. Sort lines when you plan to sort rosters and lists. Use paragraph sort when sorting notes or reports.

To sort lines

1. Retrieve a file to the screen.

2. Press Ctrl-F9 (Merge/Sort).

3. Press 2 or S to choose Sort.

4. Press Enter if you want to sort the file displayed on-screen, or type the input file name if you want to sort a file stored on disk.

5. Press Enter if you want the sorted results to replace the screen display, or type the output file name if you want the sorted results saved to disk in a new file.

6. Press 7 or T to choose Type.

7. Press 2 or L to choose Line. The title on the Sort screen is now Sort by Line, and the key location headings are Field and Word. Identify the location of key words by their Field and Word numbers in each line. Fields are separated by tabs, and words are separated by spaces.

8. After entering the key locations, press **F7** (**Exit**) to return to the main Sort and Select menu.

9. Press **1** or **P** to choose Perform Action. WordPerfect sorts the file and sends the results to the screen or to the file, as specified in Step 5.

To sort paragraphs

1. Retrieve your file to the screen if you want to perform the sort while the document is displayed.

2. Press **Ctrl-F9** (**Merge/Sort**).

3. Press **2** or **S** to choose Sort.

4. Press **Enter** if you want to sort the file displayed on-screen, or type the input file name if you want to sort a file stored on disk.

5. Press **Enter** if you want the sorted results to replace the screen display, or type the output file name if you want the sorted results saved to disk in a new file.

6. At the Sort and Select menu, press **7** or **T** to choose Type.

7. Press **3** or **P** to choose Paragraph. The heading on the main Sort screen changes to Sort by Paragraph, and the key location headings change to Line, Field, and Word. Paragraphs are separated by two or more hard returns.

8. Press **F7** (**Exit**) to return to the Sort and Select menu.

9. Press **1** or **P** for Perform Action.

Sorting Secondary Merge Files

A secondary merge file is nothing more than a database with implanted merge codes. WordPerfect can sort your secondary merge files so that the form letters, mailing lists, or labels you have previously typed will print in any order you choose.

To Sort Merge Files

1. Retrieve your file to the screen.

2. Press **Ctrl-F9 (Merge/Sort)**.

3. Press **2** or **S** to choose Sort.

4. Press **Enter** if you want to sort the file displayed on-screen, or type the input file name if you want to sort a file stored on disk.

5. Press **Enter** if you want the sorted results to replace the screen display, or type the output file name if you want the sorted results saved to disk in a new file.

6. At the Sort and Select menu, press **7** or **T** to choose Type.

7. Press **1** or **M** to choose Merge. The location headings for each key become Field, Line, and Word, and the screen heading becomes Sort Secondary Merge File.

Remember that secondary merge file records end with a ^E code and fields end with a ^R code.

8. Press **3** or **K** to choose Keys.

9. Press the right or left arrow to move between keys.

10. Press **F7 (Exit)** to return to the Sort and Select menu.

11. Press **1** or **P** to select Perform Action. WordPerfect sorts the file based on your sort criteria.

Selecting Data Precisely

When you are working with a large database, you often need to select only particular data, and you need to be precise about your selection. Using the Select feature (included in WordPerfect's Sort menu), you can choose only those paragraphs, lines, or secondary merge records that contain a specific combination of data–for example, the names of customers who live in Texas. The steps in selecting are the same as those used in sorting, except that you must include a statement that describes the records you want to select.

A simple selection statement might be:

```
Key1=perkins
```

This selection statement tells WordPerfect to select only those records in which the last name is *perkins* or *Perkins*. (WordPerfect's Sort and Select features do not distinguish between upper- and lowercase.)

Special Characters

In your documents, you may need to create special characters or type equations. WordPerfect has features that allow you to create special characters and use super- and subscripts, half-line spacing, and space fill for equations.

In most documents, only one character appears in a space. For special characters, you may want two characters to print in the same space. You can use Compose to insert one of WordPerfect's characters or to combine two characters to create one. (See the WordPerfect manual for a list of character sets.)

To create special characters with Compose

1. Press **Ctrl-2**.

2. Type the the number of the character set, a comma, and then the number of the character; then press **Enter**.

Or, if the character is a combination of two characters, type the first character, and then type the second character.

To create special characters with Overstrike

1. Move the cursor to the point where you want to create an overstrike character.

2. Press **Shift-F8 (Format)** to display the Format menu.

3. Press **4** or **O** to select Other.

4. Press **5** or **O** to select Overstrike.

5. Press **1** or **C** to choose Create.

6. Type each character (or attribute) that you want to appear in that character position.

7. Press **Enter**. As you type, you can see the characters and codes, but when you return to your document only the last character you've entered is visible.

8. Press **F7 (Exit)** to return to your document.

The characters you entered will all be printed in the same character position. To review the codes and characters, use Reveal Codes (Alt-F3 or F11).

Superscript and subscript are font attributes located on the Font: Size menu. A *superscript* is a number or letter written immediately above, or above and to the right or left, of another character. A *subscript* is a distinguishing symbol written immediately below, or below and to the right or left, of another character.

To create a subscript or superscript character

1. Press **Ctrl-F8** (**Font**).

2. Press **1** or **S** to select Size.

3. Press **1** or **P** to select Superscript, or press **2** or **B** to select Subscript.

4. Type the super- or subscripted characters.

5. Press the right-arrow key to move the cursor one character to the right when you want to return to the normal font.

If the text to be super- or subscripted is already typed, define it as a Block (Alt-F4 or F12), press the Font key (Ctrl-F8), press **1** or **S** to select Size, and then choose the appropriate appearance.

To simplify the process of entering complex formulas, you can use half-line spacing and space fill. With half-line spacing, you can enter each level of super- and subscripts on a separate line, creating several levels of super- and subscripts. Space fill creates a blank area for you to type your equation.

To create an area for entering equations

1. Position the cursor at the left margin of the first line where the equation will appear on the page.

2. Press **Shift-F8** (**Format**) to display the Format menu.

3. Press **1** or **L** to select Line.

4. Press **6** or **S** to select Line Spacing.

5. Type .5 for half-line spacing.

6. Press **Enter**.

7. If Justification (on the Format: Line menu) is set to Yes, press **3** or **J** and type **N** to turn it off.

8. Press **F7** (**Exit**) to return to your document.

9. Count the number of lines in the equation. Count subscripts, superscripts, and normal lines as separate lines.

10. Hold down the **space bar** to create a line of blank spaces. Press **Enter** at the end of each line. Create as many lines as you need. The blank spaces will make it easier to move the cursor in the equation area with the keyboard set to Typeover mode.

11. Press **Ins** to activate Typeover mode.

12. Use the **arrow keys** to move the cursor to the line where you'll type the equation.

13. Type the equation.

Spellchecking

WordPerfect's Speller contains a dictionary with more than 100,000 words. You can use the Speller to search for spelling mistakes and common typing errors such as transposed, missing, extra, or wrong letters–even typing errors such as double words (the the). You also can use the Speller when you know what a word sounds like but you're unsure of its spelling. WordPerfect's Speller will check a single word, a page, a block of text, or an entire document.

Checking Text with WordPerfect's Speller

The Speller compares each word in your document with the words in its dictionary. This dictionary contains a list of *common* words (words most frequently used) and a list of *main* words (words generally found in dictionaries). WordPerfect checks every word against its list of common words, and if the program doesn't find the word there, it looks in its dictionary of main words. If you have a supplemental dictionary, it looks there as well. Words found in any of the dictionaries are considered correct.

Reminder

If your WordPerfect program is loaded on the hard disk, the Spell files are immediately available. For the Spell function to work correctly, the files must be in the same subdirectory as WP.EXE.

To start the Speller on a dual floppy disk system

1. Be sure that you've saved in drive B the document you want to check.

2. Remove the data disk from drive B and insert your copy of the Speller disk. (Do not remove the WordPerfect Program disk from drive A.)

3. When you are finished checking spelling, put your working disk back into drive B.

To check a word, page, or entire document

1. If you plan to check just a word or a page, place the cursor anywhere in the word or page. If you plan to check the entire document, the position of the cursor does not matter.

2. If you are using a floppy disk system, remove the data disk from drive B and insert the Speller disk.

3. Press **Ctrl-F2 (Spell)**. The Spell menu appears at the bottom of the screen:

```
Check: 1 Word; 2 Page; 3 Document;
4 New Sup. Dictionary; 5 Look Up;
6 Count: 0
```

4. Press the number or letter that identifies your menu selection.

If you press **1** or **W** for Word, WordPerfect checks its dictionaries for that word. If WordPerfect finds the word, the cursor moves to the next word in your document, and the Spell menu remains displayed at the bottom of your screen. You can continue checking word-by-word or select another option from the Spell menu. If the word isn't found, WordPerfect offers alternative spellings.

If you press **2** or **P** for Page, WordPerfect looks up every word on the page. After the page is checked, the Spell menu remains displayed at the bottom of the screen. Continue checking words or select another option.

If you press **3** or **D** for Document, WordPerfect looks up every word in your document.

If you press **4** or **N** for New Sup. Dictionary, you can use a supplemental dictionary by typing the name of the dictionary and pressing Enter. Generally, these dictionaries contain words pertaining to specialized or technical areas, such as medicine, law, or science.

If you press **5** or **L** for Look Up, WordPerfect will check a word you aren't sure how to spell. In response to the Word or Word Pattern prompt, type your "rough guess" of the word's spelling. WordPerfect will offer a list of words that fit the pattern.

If you press **6** or **C** for Count, WordPerfect counts the number of words checked in a given check. If you want

to know how many words are contained in your
document, spell check the entire document or select
Count.

When the Speller finds a word not in its dictionary, the
Speller stops, highlights the word, and provides a list of
alternative spellings.

To select a word from the alternatives list

1. Find the correct spelling among the list of
   alternatives. If you do not see the correct spelling
   and WordPerfect prompts you to `Press Enter
   for More Words,` do so.

2. Type the letter next to the alternative spelling you
   want to select.

After you correct the word, the Speller continues
checking the rest of your document. WordPerfect gives
you several other options besides selecting an alternative
spelling. For a discussion of these options, see the next
section.

Using Speller Features

Many correctly spelled words do not appear in
WordPerfect's dictionary. Even with more than 100,000
words, some must be omitted. When the Speller notes a
word as incorrect, the Not Found menu is displayed:

```
Not Found: 1 Skip Once; 2 Skip; 3
Add Word; 4 Edit; 5 Look Up: 0
```

Reminders

At the Not Found menu, if you select Skip (2), the
Speller will ignore what you know to be a correctly
spelled word and continue the check. If you select Skip
Once (1), the Speller will ignore the word once, but stop
at every occurrence of the word thereafter. Skip Once
allows you to verify your spelling of the word.

If a word you use frequently is not in WordPerfect's dictionary, select Add Word (3); WordPerfect stores the word in memory and ignores all future occurrences as the spell check continues. At the end of the check, all words added are saved to the current supplemental dictionary.

When the correct alternative is not offered and when you know the spelling is incorrect, you must correct the word yourself. You can select Edit (4) and then make the necessary corrections. Or you can select Look Up (5) to display additional alternatives.

In addition to identifying misspelled words, the Speller notes double words, such as "the the." When the Speller encounters a double word, the program doesn't offer alternatives. Instead, it displays the following menu:

```
Double Word: 1 2 Skip; 3 Delete
2nd; 4 Edit; 5 Disable Double Word
Checking
```

If you accidentally typed two words instead of one, select Delete 2nd (3). Select Skip (1 or 2) if the double word is legitimate. If one of the words is a typo, select Edit (4) and make the appropriate corrections. If your document contains many legitimate double words and you are certain of your proofreading skill, select Disable Double Word Checking (5). The Speller will continue to check the rest of your text.

To edit a word

1. Press 4 or E for Edit, and the cursor moves to the word.

2. Make the corrections using the right-arrow and left-arrow keys. You can move only in the line containing the word to be corrected.

3. Press F7 (Exit). The Speller rechecks the word you've corrected. If the corrected version is not in the dictionary, the Speller stops.

To look up a word

1. Press 5 or L for Look Up. The following prompt appears on-screen:

```
Word or word pattern:
```

2. Type the word or word pattern and press Enter.

A word pattern is your guess of the word's spelling. You can type an asterisk (*) to replace an unknown number of letters or a question mark (?) to replace one unknown letter.

After you press Enter, WordPerfect displays all the possible matches. When the alternative words are displayed, you can choose one of those words to replace the not found word by pressing the letter associated with the word.

If you don't find the correct spelling among the Look Up alternatives, complete the spell check and then go back and enter the correction manually.

3. Press F7 (Exit) twice to return to your document, or enter another word or word pattern.

To check a block

1. Press Alt-F4 or F12 (Block) and define the block you want to check.

2. Press Ctrl-F2 (Spell).

When you spell check a block, you skip the Spell menu, because you've already told WordPerfect how much of your document you plan to check. Otherwise, the Speller operates as usual.

Starting WordPerfect

If you are using a dual floppy disk system

1. Insert into drive A either your 5 1/4-inch WordPerfect 1 (sys)—Working disk or your 3 1/2-inch WordPerfect 1/WordPerfect 2 (sys)—Working disk.

2. Insert a blank, formatted disk in drive B. This disk will store your documents.

3. At the DOS prompt A>, type **b:** and press **Enter** to change to drive B.

4. Type **a:wp** and press **Enter**.

5. If you have 5 1/4-inch disks, replace the disk labeled WordPerfect 1 (sys)—Working with the disk labeled WordPerfect 2 (sys)—Working.

If you are using a hard disk system

1. At the DOS prompt C>, type **cd\wp50** and press **Enter**.

2. Type **wp** and press **Enter** to start WordPerfect.

Styles

You can use Style (Alt-F8) as a powerful tool to control the format of one document or a group of documents. A style is a group of WordPerfect codes (you can include text also) that you turn on and off to control the format of your document. Styles save time by reducing the number of formatting keystrokes. For example, a style may contain all the codes needed to format a chapter heading, or a long quotation. Style definitions are saved with the current document, or you can save them to a style library file to use on other documents.

WordPerfect's styles fall into two categories: *open* and *paired*. Open styles remain in effect until you override the style codes, either by using another style or by inserting other formatting codes manually. Use open styles for formatting that affects an entire document. For instance, use open styles to set margins, tabs, line spacing, hyphenation, and so forth. If the style is to affect the entire document, move the cursor to the beginning of the document before turning on the style.

Paired styles are turned on and off. You can create a paired style called Heading that makes the text bold and italic. When you use this style, you insert [Style On: Heading] and [Style Off: Heading] codes around the text to be formatted. Use paired styles for titles, section headings, tables–any text element that has a beginning and an end.

To use a style

1. Move the cursor to where you want the style to begin.

2. Press **Alt-F8** (**Style**) to display the Styles menu.

3. Use the cursor keys to highlight the style you want to use.

4. Press **1** or **O** or **Enter** to turn on the style.

5. Type your text.

If you are using a paired style and defined Enter as Off, the style is turned off when you press Enter. If you are using a paired style and defined Enter as HRt or On/Off, to turn off the style, press Alt-F8 (Style) and press **2** or **F**.

To use a paired style with existing text, press Alt-F4, or F12 (Block), highlight the text, then follow Steps 1–4 for using a style.

When you save your document, the style definitions are saved with your document regardless of whether you used them or not. Whenever you edit this document, the styles are available for use. You also can save style definitions to a style library; then you can use these styles on other documents.

You can use the style library (LIBRARY.STY) found on WordPerfect's Conversion disk, or you can create a style library yourself. Also, you can set up one style library as your default.

Tab Stops

WordPerfect 5 comes with tab stops predefined at one-half inch intervals. Four basic kinds of tabs are available: left, center, right, and decimal. In addition, each type of tab can have a *dot leader* (a series of dots before the tab). The following table explains the types of tabs available.

Tab Type	*Operation*
Left (L)	Indent to tab stop; text continues right. Left tab is the most commonly used tab stop.
Center (C)	Text is centered at tab stop. Center tab works much the same as Shift-F6 (Center) except the center tab can force centering anywhere on the line, not just the center between margins. Center tabs are used to create column headings.
Right (R)	After a right tab stop, text continues to the left. Right tab stop is similar to Alt-F6 (Flush Right), except right tab stops can be placed anywhere on the line, not just at the right margin.

Right tab can be used to create headings over columns of numbers and dates.

Decimal (D)   After a decimal tab stop, text continues to the left until the alignment character is typed, then text continues to the right. Decimal tab stops are similar to Ctrl-F6 (Tab Align) except you preset the alignment character as a tab stop. The default alignment character is a period (.), but you can change it to any character (, :, $, for example). Use decimal tabs to line up columns of numbers.

Dot Leaders (.)   Any of the four tab types can be preceded by dots (periods) as leaders. Use dot leaders for long lists that require scanning from left to right (phone lists, for instance).

You can change tab settings for all documents or for only the document upon which you're currently working. When you change the settings for your current document only, the settings affect only the text from the point at which you make the change.

You can set tab stops one at a time, or you can specify the increment and set several tab stops at once. Similarly, you can delete one tab stop, all tab stops, or only the tab stops to the right of the cursor. You can set multiple tab stops across 8.5 inches of your page. If you print on wider paper, you can extend tab stops from 8.5 inches to 54.5 inches, but you must set those stops individually. You can set a maximum of 40 tab stops.

To view current tab stop settings, use the Window feature to display the tab ruler at the bottom of your screen.

═══════════════════════════════

To display the tab ruler

1. Press **Ctrl-F3** (**Screen**).

2. Press **1** or **W** for Window. The following prompt appears, followed by a number:

```
Number of lines in this window:
```

The number which follows the colon depends on the type of monitor you have or the number you entered for the /ss start-up option when you loaded WordPerfect.

3. Type a number that is one less than the one displayed in the prompt.

4. Press **Enter**.

A tab ruler appears at the bottom of your screen. The curly braces, { and }, mark the left and right margins. (Instead of braces you may see brackets, [and]. The brackets indicate that the tab stops have been changed from their original values.) The triangles mark the tab stops.

To erase the tab ruler repeat Steps 1 and 2. For Step 3, type a number one greater than the value displayed in the prompt.

═══════════════════════════════

To change the tab stops

1. Press **Shift-F8** (**Format**).

2. Press **1** or **L** to display the Format: Line menu.

3. Press **8** or **T** to select Tab Set and to display the tab ruler.

4. *To delete a single tab stop,* use the cursor keys to move to the tab you want to delete and press **Del** or **Backspace** to delete the tab.

To delete all tab stops, move the cursor to the left margin by pressing **Home, Home,** ← ; then press **Ctrl-End**.

To delete tab stops to the right of the cursor, type the number (in inches) of the first tab stop you want to delete, press **Enter**, and then press **Ctrl-End**.

5. *To add a single tab stop,* use the cursor keys to move to the position where you want a tab stop and press the appropriate tab type: **L** to add a left tab, **C** to add a center tab, **R** to add a right tab, or **D** to add a decimal tab. To add a dot leader, press **.** (period).

To add multiple left tab stops, type the number of inches to mark the location where tabs will begin, a comma, and the spacing increment; then, press **Enter**. For example, to space tabs one-half inch apart beginning at one inch, type **1,.5** and press **Enter**.

To add multiple center, right, or decimal tab stops and dot leaders, use the cursor keys to move the cursor to the position where you want tab stops to begin. Press **C** (Center), **R** (Right), or **D** (Decimal). If you want a dot leader, press **.** (period). Then type the number of inches to mark the location where the tab stops are to begin, a comma, and the spacing increment; press **Enter**. For example, to space right-aligned tab stops one-half inch apart beginning at one inch, position the cursor at one inch, press **R**, type **1,.5**, and then press **Enter**.

6. Press **F7** (**Exit**) twice to return to your document.

Tables of Authorities

The term *table of authorities* may be unfamiliar unless you work with legal briefs or scholarly manuscripts. A table of authorities is a list of court cases, rules of court, statutes, agency opinions, and miscellaneous authorities mentioned in a document. Each type of authority is usually assigned its own section in the table. Within each section, the citations are listed alphabetically, with page references.

Your table of authorities can contain up to 16 sections. You enter the first reference (or *full form*) of the authority in a special editing screen. Then, if there are subsequent references to the same citation, you give these a unique *short form* identifier so that WordPerfect can collect these subsequent references and compile them in a table with their page references. You can mark authorities in footnotes, endnotes, and graphics boxes, as well as in the body text.

Once you've marked the authorities, you need to enter a definition code that tells WordPerfect where, and in what format, to generate the table of authorities.

Each section of a table of authorities is alphabetized separately; therefore, you can set up separate lists of case citations, constitutional citations, and legal citations. You must define each section separately.

For a thorough coverage of the Table of Authorities feature—the rules and guidelines for creating and using this option—read Chapter 22 in *Using WordPerfect 5*.

Tables of Contents

When you create a table of contents, WordPerfect generally uses text taken directly from the document—chapter headings, for example. Creating a table of contents is similar to generating an index: first, you mark the text to be included in the table of contents; then, define the style; and finally, generate the table of contents.

WordPerfect inserts a [Mark:ToC,1] code at the beginning of the marked text, and an [End Mark:ToC,1] code at the end. To omit the marked item from the table of contents, delete one code; WordPerfect deletes the other code for you. Formatting codes (underline and boldface codes, for example) are included in the table of contents if you include them when you mark the text.

You can change any or all of the following options:

Number of Levels: Select this option, type the number of levels you want to include in your table of contents, and press Enter.

Display Last Level in Wrapped Format: Choose this option and press Y if you want to display the last level of the table of contents in wrapped format. Press N if you don't want this option turned on.

Select Page Number Position: Use this option to specify one of the following page number positions for each of your levels: None, Pg # Follows, (Pg #) Follows, Flush Rt, Flush Rt with Leader. (You may not choose a flush-right style for the last level if you've specified that the line will word-wrap.)

When you define the table of contents, WordPerfect enters a code in your document that reflects the options you've selected—for example, [Def Mark:ToC,3:4,5,5]. The table of contents will be generated at this mark.

To generate a table of contents, press **Alt-F5** (**Mark Text**) and follow the prompts.

The Thesaurus

The Thesaurus is similar to the Speller, except that the Thesaurus contains *synonyms*—words with the same or similar meanings—and *antonyms*—words with opposite or nearly opposite meanings. The Thesaurus only lists these words; you must decide which one most closely fits your meaning. If you are not certain of the correct spelling, use the asterisk (*) and the question mark (?) to check the word, and then use the Thesaurus.

When using the Thesaurus, the word you look up is called the *headword* because it has a body of similar words attached to it. The headword appears at the top of the column. Synonyms and antonyms for your headword are noted with a bullet. Remember that words marked with a bullet also are headwords; you can look up any of these words for more ideas.

To use the Thesaurus
1. If you are using a floppy disk system, remove the data disk from drive B and insert the Thesaurus disk. The WordPerfect Program disk must remain in drive A.

If you are using a hard disk system, copy the Thesaurus disk files into the WordPerfect directory.

2. Place the cursor anywhere in the word you want to look up and press **Alt-F1** (**Thesaurus**).

If your menu is empty and Word: appears at the bottom
of your screen, either the cursor was not placed within
the word boundary or the Thesaurus cannot find the
word you want to look up. In either case, type the word
you want to look up at the Word: prompt and press
Enter.

3. To replace the highlighted word, press **1** (Replace
   Word). The following prompt appears on-screen:

   ```
   Press letter for word
   ```

4. Type the letter that corresponds to the replacement
   word. The Thesaurus menu disappears, and the
   program inserts into the text the word you selected.

5. If you are using a floppy disk system, remove the
   Thesaurus disk, replace it with your data disk, and
   save your document.

To view other words

1. Press **Alt-F1** (**Thesaurus**).

2. Press **3** for Look Up Word.

3. After the Word: prompt, type the word you want
   to look up. If the word is a headword, the Thesaurus
   displays the word with all its subgroups of
   synonyms and antonyms. If the word is not a
   headword, WordPerfect either looks up another
   similar word or displays the message * Word
   Not Found *. You can either press **F1** (**Cancel**)
   or look up another word.

Upper- and Lowercase

WordPerfect can change whole words, sentences, paragraphs, or documents to upper- or lowercase automatically. This feature is useful when, for example, you discover that you've typed a section of text with Caps Lock turned on.

To Change to Upper- or Lowercase Letters

1. Position the cursor at the beginning of the section of text to be changed.

2. Press Alt-F4 (Block). The following message appears on your screen:

   ```
   Block on
   ```

3. Move the cursor to the end of the text you want to change.

4. Press Shift-F3 (Switch).

5. Press 1 or U to change to uppercase letters, or press 2 or L to change from uppercase to lowercase letters.

After the highlighted text changes case, the Switch menu disappears.

Note

Because WordPerfect recognizes the first word of a sentence and the pronoun "I," they remain capitalized when you select lowercase. To ensure that WordPerfect recognizes that the block is a sentence, include the previous sentence's ending punctuation when you define your block of text.

Windows

WordPerfect gives you two "sheets of paper" to work on at once if you choose to do so. WordPerfect's two document "windows" give you essentially two areas within which to work. The status line tells you whether the Doc 1 or the Doc 2 window is the "active" work space. The cursor's position determines whether the window is active.

You can type in both windows and switch back and forth between them with ease. Initially, each window is the entire size of the screen. You can even split the screen to look at two documents or at different parts of the same document at once.

Reminders

When you display two documents at once, you "lose" two lines of the screen. These "lost" lines are used by an additional status line, as well as a ruler line.

Before you split the screen, decide how many lines you want to display in the current document. The other document will take what is left.

To switch between document windows:

1. Press **Shift-F3 (Switch)**. The status line should display Doc 2. If text is in the Doc 1 window, don't worry—it hasn't been lost.

2. To switch back to the Doc 1 window, press **Shift-F3 (Switch)** again.

To split the screen

1. Press **Ctrl-F3 (Screen)**. The following menu is displayed:

```
0 Rewrite; 1 Window;
2 Line Draw: 0
```

2. Press **1** (**Window**). The following prompt appears on the status line:

```
Number of lines in this window: 24
```

3. Type **11**, and then press **Enter**.

Your screen should be split in half, with WordPerfect's tab ruler line displayed across the middle.

To resize the window to a full-screen display

1. Press **Ctrl-F3** (**Screen**).

2. Select **1** or **W** for Window.

3. At the prompt asking for the number of lines in the window, type **24** and press **Enter**.

The window is now a full-screen display.

Word Search

WordPerfect 5 offers several useful ways to locate specific text. One of the most powerful is Word Search from the List Files (F5) menu. Greatly expanded from previous WordPerfect versions, Word Search searches through disk files for a given word or phrase that may be located on the first page, somewhere within the document, or in a document summary. Generally, you should try to limit a word search to only those files that meet special conditions.

Using the Word Search Command

To define Word Search conditions

1. Press **F5** (**List Files**).

2. At the `Dir` prompt, enter a directory name to display all the files in a given directory.

3. Mark the files you want to include in the search by moving the cursor to the file name and pressing the asterisk (*) key. If you want to search all files, omit this step.

4. At the List Files screen, press **9** or **W** to choose Word Search. WordPerfect displays the Search menu:

```
Search: 1 Doc Summary; 2 First
Page; 3 Entire Doc; 4 Conditions:
```

5. To search only the document summaries of the marked files, press **1** or **D** to choose Doc Summary. WordPerfect prompts:

```
Word pattern:
```

6. Type a single word or a word pattern.

7. Press **Enter** to start the search.

When the search is completed, the names of files in which the word pattern is located are displayed in a List Files screen marked with an asterisk. If no files contain the word pattern, a Not Found message is displayed, and no files on the List Files screen are marked with asterisks.

To move the cursor forward and backward from one marked file to another, use Tab and Shift-Tab, respectively.

8. To view a marked file, move the cursor to the file name on the List Files screen, and then press **6** or **L** for Look. WordPerfect displays the text of the document whose name you've highlighted in the List Files screen.

9. To return to the List Files menu from the Word Search menu, keeping the same files marked after using Look, press **F7** (**Exit**).

10. Press **F7** (**Exit**) again to leave List Files. If you retrieve a file and want to return to the List Files screen with the same files still marked, press List Files twice.

To search only the first page of the marked files

1. Repeat Steps 1–4 in the preceding steps for defining Word Search conditions.

2. At the Search menu, press **2** or **F** to choose First Page.

3. Repeat Steps 6–10 in the steps for defining Word Search conditions.

To search the entire text of each file you've marked

1. Repeat Steps 1–4 in the steps for defining Word Search conditions.

2. At the Search menu, press **3** or **E** to choose Entire Doc.

3. Repeat Steps 6–10 in the steps for defining Word Search conditions.

Using Wild Cards To Search with Word Patterns

When you conduct a word search and WordPerfect prompts you to enter a word pattern (see Step 5 in the steps for defining Word Search conditions), you can use special wild-card characters. A question mark (?) represents a single character, and an asterisk (*) represents any number of characters up to a hard return. These are some examples of allowable word patterns:

Word Pattern	Description
duck	WordPerfect finds files that contain the word *duck*.
d?ck	WordPerfect finds files that contain *duck*, *deck*, *Dick*, or *dock*.
d*k	WordPerfect finds files containing *duck*, *damask*, and *Derek*.
ducks can	WordPerfect finds files that contain such phrases as *ducks can waddle*, and *ducks cannot stand on their heads*.
ducks*can	WordPerfect finds files that contain such text as *Ducks have adapted to many environments. They can*

Upper- and lowercase letters are treated the same. In this respect, Word Search differs from WordPerfect's Search functions (F2 and Shift-F2), which match capitalized letters in a search string. If you entered *Duck*, Search would not stop at *duck*, but Word Search would mark files that contained either *duck* or *Duck*.